Inclusive Design for Organisations

Including your **missing 20%** by embedding
web and mobile accessibility

Prof. Jonathan Hassell

RETHINK PRESS

Praise

'For someone who is looking to begin the process
of implementing accessibility practice into their
organisation, I see this volume as essential.'

> – **Jennison Asuncion**, Head of
> Accessibility Engineering Evangelism,
> LinkedIn and Founder of the Global
> Accessibility Awareness Day

'Jonathan Hassell is one of the shining lights of the
global digital accessibility campaign. Now, with his
own company, Hassell Inclusion, he has done the
very thing many professionals dread doing: he has
taken the time and effort to put everything he knows
into a book so that anyone with influence over the
way digital systems are designed can ensure disabled
people are included in the digital future. This is not a
dry, difficult read; the writing is human, personable
and from the perspective of one who understands

the challenges ahead, but believes a better future is well within our collective grasp. Congratulations, Jonathan, for bringing this important book into being. I hope it gets the wide readership it deserves.'

– **Julie Howell**, Lead Author of PAS 78

'This is an outstanding resource. I can't wait to start embedding the advice in this book into my daily work flow. I've done a lot of work within accessibility, but this definitely helps bring me to another level.'

– **Chris Loiselle**, Accessibility Team Lead, Perkins School for the Blind and Invited Expert W3C

'A book that should be on the shelf of every head designer or strategist of any company that sells a product or government agency that seeks to include all of its employees and constituents. Jonathan Hassell spent hundreds of hours interviewing the leaders in this field. They are, like Hassell, passionate about their involvement in taking on the limitations imposed by the digital environment for people who need alternative access. Their enthusiasm quickly becomes your own. Their solutions are shared freely, for your benefit – you can use them for your own business or agency. Whatever your corporate task is related to accessibility, there will be a chapter and practical information on how to implement small and big changes that make a difference.'

> – **Elianna James**, Director of Accessibility Training, Be Accessible Inc.

'I want you to imagine for a moment that Professor Jonathan Hassell's *Including your missing 20% by embedding web and mobile accessibility* is like a large set of well-labelled keys. Each chapter is part of that key set and enables the reader, whether expert or layperson, to unlock the power of BS8878, the British Standard on Web Accessibility. If your organisation is looking to embed web accessibility from the outset or to adopt best practice, then you need go no further: this book is for you.'

> – **Neil Rogers**, PhD candidate, University of Southampton

Contents

Foreword

Disability inclusion is an opportunity for every organisation to assure full access to all customers. Inclusive design allows designers to create designs that are innovative, creative and functional. These design efforts benefit everyone, including people with disabilities. People with disabilities are a significant force in society; historically underappreciated, but thanks to societal shifts and technology, this community is an emerging global economic force.

Adopting an inclusive, accessible and universal design approach to technology is a smart strategy for public and private organisations wishing to proactively adjust to the future needs of this growing population. Many countries have legislation to protect the rights of persons with disabilities, resulting from the United Nations Convention on the Rights of Persons with Disabilities (CRPD). By recognising the importance of the protection and promotion of the rights and dignity of persons with disabilities through provision of innovative assistive technologies and accessible ICTs, corporations can better ensure the full inclusion of individuals in the workforce and in society.

While accessible websites and apps are great enablers, they can also present important challenges for corporations when accessibility requirements are not met. Bodies like W3C WAI have created standards to address accessibility and disability inclusion. There are also many accessibility consultants working within corporations and providing services through specialist agencies working to help implement those standards. Yet corporations and organisations often tell me that they are confused about accessibility, inclusive design and disability inclusion.

I have worked in the accessibility field since 2001 and have created several technology firms focused on inclusive design, accessibility and disability inclusion. Living in the United States but travelling extensively across the world and consulting with the United Nations has given me a bird's eye view of corporate brands interacting with the community of persons with disabilities. It has not been a fun journey for many corporations trying to comply with laws regarding disability inclusion, ICT accessibility and barrier removal that have been in place for almost thirty years.

Corporations want to be accessible, but the standards and legislation are often confusing, hard to adopt, impossible to keep in compliance with, and difficult to embed across the organisation.

As a result, corporations are increasingly being sued. This is a global trend: in China, the United Kingdom, Australia or Hungary, advocates bring cases of inaccessible websites, telephone services or bank ATMs to court. And in the United States, the Department of Justice is increasing its pressure on large organisations to align their websites with web accessibility standards. Lawsuits are on the rise. In 2018, according to an analysis by international legal firm Seyfarth Shaw, the number of federal lawsuits filed in response to web inaccessibility was almost three times higher than the year before, going from 814 to 2,285. And, while some corporations are getting the hang of web accessibility, lawyers are now branching out to look at the accessibility of mobile apps and apps on the growing number of new internet-enabled devices.

Corporations are at the crossroads of compliance pressures, human rights, citizenship considerations and market opportunities.

I have been following Professor Jonathan Hassell's impressive work for many years, and often recommend that my clients read his blogs, articles and the first edition of this book.

The British Standard BS 8878, of which he led the creation, always intrigued me, because it offers a potential solution to these issues that I see every day. It sets out practical ways of embedding accessibility within organisations' policies and processes to ensure they deliver accessibility in a sustainable way. It allows organisations to test the way they make products accessible, as well as the products themselves. Now ISO has launched ISO 30071-1 – the international version of the British Standard – organisations globally have a blueprint for making it easier to finally implement and manage accessibility.

This book explains in detail, and with excellent examples from around the world, why digital inclusion and accessibility makes good business sense, and how to implement it, blending accessibility responsibilities across the entire organisation. And, while most books on this topic only address accessibility from the perspective of websites, this book, like the ISO standard, understands that all technology needs to be made accessible. It is essential to embed accessible software development lifecycle processes for all products, apps and services, across all digital devices. This updated second edition of the book shows you how to do just that.

– **Debra Ruh**
CEO, Ruh Global IMPACT
Co-founder, AXSChat

Preface To The Second Edition

Inclusive design is now cool. It's 'so hot right now'.

In LinkedIn's '50 Big Ideas for 2019', inclusive design was number 6, just below Brexit, just above artificial intelligence (AI). And don't just take their word for it. Take Satya Nadella's, or Tim Cook's, or any of the other senior execs talking about it at the likes of Google, IBM or Facebook.

According to Satya Nadella, '2019 is the year inclusive design goes mainstream'.

Why?

Inclusive design is a new way of talking about accessibility, which accessibility advocates have been talking about for decades. So, what has suddenly made it so exciting, rather than something many people do because they feel they have to? If tech giants like Apple and Microsoft are investing in it heavily, should you too? What are the benefits for you in your organisation – whether you're a retailer that uses the web for selling what you make, a marketing agency creating mobile apps for clients, or a tiny not-for-profit promoting yourself on social media?

Accessibility advocates are thrilled that inclusive design is now getting all this attention. But some people are rightly asking if it's here for the long term, or if it's just a fad. If you invest lots of money in it now, will it be the best decision you made this year, or something you'll regret in a few years?

These are the right questions to be asking right now. I'd suggest the people answering them should be those who've been working towards becoming mature in digital accessibility for almost twenty years now. People who've been through the learning curve, made the mistakes and learnt from them, so you don't have to. People like those who gathered together at ISO and BSI to put their experience into ISO 30071-1, and BS 8878 before that. People who read the first edition of this book in 2014 and have been getting good at this ever since.

I believe this book, and its companion *Inclusive Design for Products*, which together explain ISO 30071-1, are a great way to understand the value of inclusive design for your organisation and embed it into your thinking, culture, policies and product processes. I hope it helps your organisation become inclusive in a way that doesn't cost you the earth, so you can start enjoying the benefits of inclusive design for your market segment and product type.

– **Jonathan Hassell**

ONE

Introduction

Most organisations are oblivious to, or terrified about, digital accessibility.

They're probably aware that up to 20% of their customers – people with disabilities – could be clicking away from their websites or leaving their mobile apps every day, without having bought anything or found the information or service they wished to find, never to return. They may even have heard from some of this 20%, complaining about problems they can't understand, asking for what seem like impossible fixes when their teams are already overloaded with much-needed new feature development. They know there's the possibility they'll be sued if they don't do the right thing, but they don't know how far they need to go to prevent that.

While some tech giants are investing in inclusive design, they don't know if there's anything in it for them other than risk mitigation against laws that seem to be constantly changing, that don't line up internationally, and for which they can find precious little case law to constitute a credible legal threat (unless they are in the United States). They're anxious to know what their competitors are doing, whether this is an area in which they should be a leader or follower, and what the value of accessibility would be – possibly as a unique selling point (USP) – if they invested in it. Their web teams may have read the industry standard Web Content Accessibility Guidelines (WCAG) but found them impenetrable and badly organised. Worse, when their designers do locate the 'success criteria' for design, the guidelines seem like a creative straitjacket that tells them everything they can't do, but little about why.

Accessibility, it seems, is a cul-de-sac that organisations are being legally blackmailed into spending time on, which will result in products that are better for the 20% of people with disabilities and worse for the 80% who are not disabled. Moreover, they have no idea how many disabled people are actually using their site or app, or how many more will because they're now spending good money making it more accessible. So, if they do make something 'accessible', it's usually only for one product or one version of a product. And it's usually because of one committed, passionate 'accessibility superhero' on the team whose departure would leave them needing to start all over again.

If this sounds like where you work, I have some comforting news: you are not alone.

I learnt where I believe most organisations want to be directly from the heads of diversity and inclusion of the top blue-chip corporations in Europe at a meeting of the Vanguard Network early in 2011. I was speaking for the BBC at the event on the innovation possibilities of web accessibility for inclusion, but before I could start, the event's chair did something amazing. She spent a whole hour going around the room, asking each of the delegates what one thing would really make a difference to their organisation's inclusion practices if they could achieve it. When they were asked to vote for which of the contributions each felt was the most important, this was the unanimous choice:

> 'What I want is to strategically embed inclusion into my organisation's culture and business-as-usual processes, rather than just doing *another* inclusion project.'

If you were sitting opposite me at the event, you'd have seen my mouth open wide in recognition: the British standard that I and so many other people had laboured on for three years was exactly what those in the room were asking for, at least when it came to their organisation's digital presence.

I spent much of my lunchtime conveying to the people in the room that:

- They could implement a strategy that would allow them to attract and keep the 20% of their audience who are disabled, while not detracting from the user experience of those who aren't

- There was a way they could sleep soundly, knowing that they'd done enough to cover their 'accessibility risk' without it costing the earth

- Through following a simple, strategic business-aligned framework, they could embed the best practice necessary to *consistently* achieve these aims throughout their organisation and digital products

- The framework would allow them to align accessibility and usability within their product teams, showing them when both could be achieved together and when the user needs of different groups would require them to add personalisation to their products

- All of this work could benefit their organisation, not just in risk mitigation, customer service and

corporate social responsibility, but also in their
bottom line as benchmarked analytics show how
disabled and older people's use of their sites
could increase their turnover and profits

What did I have that could take these people's
organisations from their position of pain to the
place they all wanted to be? The standard that I'd
just led the creation of for the British Standards
Institution (BSI). British Standard (BS) 8878:2010 *Web
Accessibility – Code of Practice.* BS 8878 opened up
in detail the strategies, policies and processes that
award-winning, best-of-breed organisations like the
BBC, IBM, Vodafone, Opera, BT and Lloyds Banking
Group have used to become 'accessibility competent
and confident' so that they can be used by any
organisation, no matter how big or small.

One month later, I was at a conference of
international accessibility standards experts at BSI
in London, chatting with people from Japan and
Canada who told me that they had an immediate
need for the standard in their countries. These
conversations took me on an eight-year journey to
deliver what they were asking for – *ISO 30071-1,*
which is the internationalisation and extension of BS
8878. It was launched in May 2019, prompting the
second edition of this book.

ISO 30071-1 has arrived at a time when some of the largest companies on the planet – including Apple, Google and Microsoft – are recognising that inclusive design is an idea that needs to go mainstream. Tablet and smartphone vendors are racing to promote accessibility as a key selling point of their devices. The legal imperatives behind accessibility are being strengthened internationally and the number of cases being brought against inaccessible websites is rising at a huge rate.

We are also entering a massive demographic change as baby boomers all over the world start to need some of the same accessibility features that disabled people have always needed. As our populations age, the number of people who need accessibility is rocketing up – the 'missing 20%' is rapidly becoming 'the missing 40%'.

There's never been a better time to get good at digital accessibility, especially as people who have embedded BS 8878 in their production processes are increasingly telling me that its user-centred inclusive design thinking has resulted in not only *more* *accessible* websites and apps for disabled people, but *better* websites and apps for everyone. On top of that, I have numerous stories of how the inclusive design thinking in BS 8878 and ISO 30071-1 has helped organisations be more innovative in their product ideation, which is why I was in the room with the Vanguard Network in the first place.

So I'm hoping you, like the Vanguard Network, will want to know more...

Note on language

You'll find I interchange between the words 'accessibility' and 'inclusion' throughout this book. I will sometimes use 'accessibility' as it's the word most people know, but I prefer 'inclusion' as it avoids one of the main pitfalls that people who care about ensuring those with disabilities are not excluded can fall into: they care so much about how easy it is for people with disabilities to use products, they forget about the needs of people without disabilities using the same product. For them, accessibility is the *most* important aspect of the product, not *an* important aspect of the product.

I believe sacrificing the needs of the majority non-disabled audience to uphold the needs of the minority of people with disabilities is always the wrong thing to do. It's unsustainable. It doesn't allow *everyone* to win. It just swaps the people who win from being people without disabilities to being people with disabilities.

That's not a good enough goal. The goal should always be to make products work for everyone, rather than saying that's the goal, and then acting like disabled audiences are more important than any other audience, spurred on by guidelines that don't take the impact of every checkpoint on non-disabled users and project budgets adequately into account.

Inclusive design or 'universal design' is at the heart of ISO 30071-1. It reminds everyone to consider *all* user groups. And it benefits all user groups, because when it asks digital product owners to think about people with disabilities who are so different from themselves, they become sensitive to the needs of people who are only a little different to themselves – ageing parents, for example. Going the extra mile makes them more sensitive to everyone's needs, which can only be a good thing.

Support materials to accompany this book

This book contains many important lessons that some of the world's most successful accessibility experts learnt when they embedded a framework for accessibility competence in their organisation. To help you put their advice into practice in your organisation, I've created a wealth of free resources to help you complete the practical exercises I've included at the end of most sections of the book:

- Tools and templates that you can use to quickly get started with

    - Generating a tailored accessibility business case for your organisation

    - Creating your organisational information and communications technology (ICT) accessibility policy

    - Creating ICT system accessibility logs for your digital products

    - Prioritising issues that get uncovered by accessibility testing

- Access to Hassell Inclusion's latest podcasts and blogs, which are refreshed weekly

- Information on training, webinars and support forums

This book is just the start. Get help for the rest of your journey from http://qrs.ly/3a4a6bm or use the QR code below:

TWO

The Hassell Inclusion Way Of Implementing ISO 30071-1

L et's start with an overview of the different stages of the journey towards digital accessibility competence and confidence that most organisations could benefit from.

At Hassell Inclusion, we call these the Five Keys to unlock solutions to critical elements of digital accessibility maturity:

1. *Expand awareness* – expanding your thinking about how your organisation can benefit from inclusive design

2. *Embed strategy* – embedding inclusion as a value and competence across all parts of your organisation, so all your staff and policies are working together to gain you those benefits

3. *Enable process* – enabling your digital production teams to create products that are inclusive by embedding accessibility in their process

4. *Measure effects* – measuring the effect all of this has on your organisation's users/customers, brand reputation and bottom line

5. *Continually evolve* – planning how to evolve your accessibility thinking and practice as technology changes, and how you can evolve technology yourself through innovations that come from engaging with different people's access needs

I will go into detail on each of these stages in the following chapters, but for now I want to introduce each by way of a real-world story.

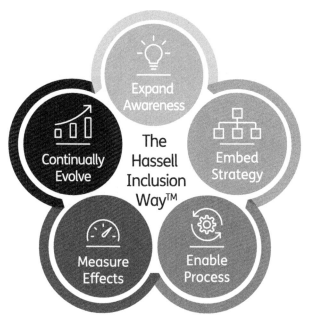

The Five Keys to The Hassell Inclusion Way

Expand awareness

It's critical to use the first key before you go any
further in your journey towards accessibility
competence and confidence. If you don't expand
your thinking, your whole organisation will
be unsure of the reasoning behind the training,
governance, policies or processes you introduce.
You'll be taking your staff on a journey that will
involve them learning new skills, working in new
ways and changing 'the way things are done around

here' without telling them why any change is necessary, what the point of the change is and when it will be over. Even worse, your organisation may start on a journey because 'that's what everyone else is doing' and end up in the wrong destination because it is actually different from 'everyone else'.

The first key is expanding your thinking about why you should go on the journey at all – examining the reasons and motivations for doing it to find which best fit your organisation's culture, purposes and products or services.

There are lots of good reasons for behaving in a certain way, but if you're unsure of your motivation, you will be forever second-guessing how you should behave when the journey gets difficult.

Let me tell you a story.

Have you ever been in a traffic jam?

Imagine me in my 2002-model blue Ford Focus – the most inclusively designed car of all time – at 11.15 on a crisp morning in January. I'm just coming out of a traffic jam that has been frustrating me for the last thirty minutes. But finally, the road ahead looks clear.

I should be feeling relieved.

Today is my mother's birthday – that's the reason why my family and I are on this motorway. And it's the reason why I'm still frustrated, because between me and the clear road ahead is a figure that is stressing me out. The figure is one of the main reasons why I bought my satnav. It's the one thing that no satnav will ever be sold without.

It's the estimated time of arrival (ETA).

My mother's birthday lunch is booked for 12.15. The ETA says 12.30.

So, what does my right foot do?

Five minutes later, another aspect of my satnav comes into play – the speed-camera detection, which shows me a camera is coming up. Why is this a problem? Because I'm not going at the speed limit, like pretty much every other car I can see on the road. So I slow down. But for how long? Ten minutes? One minute? No, more like fifteen seconds. Because as soon as I'm past the camera, my right foot takes over again.

Why this behaviour? Why am I not going at the speed limit when everything says that I should? The law says that I should be going slower. I know it's the 'right thing to do' – it would be better for the environment, and safer for my wife and son sitting in the back of the car. It would even be cheaper for me, over time helping me save money which I could spend on whatever I wanted...

But no, all of these motivations are outweighed by my ETA. That's what's driving me. Anything else is a distraction I'll work around.

Compare this situation with the roads in Norway. If my colleagues at an accessibility conference in Oslo are correct, there the authorities seem to actually understand human behaviour. In Norway, speed cameras take photos of all the cars that go past them, not just those that are speeding, because you don't pay your speeding fines to a faceless bureaucrat in a government office somewhere; you pay them to the people who were going under the speed limit past the same speed camera on the same day.

In Norway, a speed camera can be your friend. It can even make you money. You can win.

So, where would you prefer to drive? England? Or Norway?

That's just a simple example to show why it's necessary to reframe the accessibility conversation. For too long, digital accessibility has been considered to be all about avoiding losing. All about getting away with as little as possible, doing only what you absolutely have to do to avoid getting into legal trouble. Riding your luck. The best thing that could happen is that you successfully get away with ignoring it, because there's nothing to win. Buying the cheapest accessibility insurance policy you can, because you're not convinced that you'll ever need it.

That's not motivational to anyone other than your risk management department.

To be worth doing at all, accessibility needs to be considered in the right way. With 20 to 40% of your potential audience caring about how you handle the accessibility of your products, it isn't about avoiding losing, it's about winning. Winning a bigger audience. Winning better brand reputation. Just plain old winning.

Now that sounds far more interesting, doesn't it?

Chapter 3 will allow you to expand the way you think about accessibility so that you can understand its *relative importance* to your organisation, when compared with all the other aspects of product design, so you have a stable, reliable motivation for spending time on it.

Embed strategy

Once you've expanded your thinking to encompass better motivation for accessibility, the second key is critical to ensure that you can actually *deliver it* in the culture and structure of your organisation. This is about identifying all the things that need to work together to make sure you deliver the accessibility you want efficiently, and that nothing snatches defeat from the jaws of success.

I'm talking about embedding inclusion as a value that pervades your organisation. Like a stick of seaside rock, a cross section of any aspect of your organisation should show the same values at play. Not only is there nothing there that could derail your ability to deliver to your values, but there is understanding, competence and confidence present that this is not only worth doing, but is also achievable.

To give you an analogy from a sport I took up after I was spurred on by Britain's successes in the 2012 London Olympics, let's consider how rowing teams win.

Firstly, everyone in the boat has the same goal – to go in the same direction as quickly as possible.

There's not much chance for an individual rower to do otherwise with only one oar in their hands, but they could turn the oar over and try and push the water the other way if they wanted to slow the whole team down. And yes, a couple of times on my early outings in the boat, a number of us novices inadvertently ended up doing just that. Not because we wanted to, but because we were concentrating on another part of our stroke at the time.

Secondly, everyone in the boat is doing their job, not someone else's. There are effectively three jobs in the boat: the one 'stroke' rower is establishing the rowers' rhythm; the other seven rowers are rowing to that rhythm; and the one cox is steering and providing feedback to each rower on how they need to tweak their performance to stick to that rhythm. If two people try to steer the boat, say by stopping rowing on one side so the boat turns against its rudder, it's fighting against itself. If a rower who isn't 'stroke' decides to set a different rhythm, say by rowing faster to make the boat go faster, this actually slows the boat down and confuses the whole crew. If an inexperienced or lower-skilled rower doesn't pay attention to feedback from the cox on how they are rowing, an unchecked increase in the depth their blade goes into the water could unbalance the boat and end up rocking it up and down, resulting in the

other rowers needing to work to stabilise it rather
than concentrating on powering forwards.

Thirdly, the equipment the team is using could
sabotage the enterprise. A great crew, harmonised in
purpose, rhythm and technique, can be beaten by a
group of novices if there's a leak in the boat.

And finally, a winning team can slowly go off the boil
if they feel that the club they row for is taking them
for granted. They may feel that new club leaders are
more interested in other parts of running the club,
assuming that the team will always win even if they
aren't given the time to practise or feedback on any
bad habits that might be creeping into their game.

The same is true for any organisation – for it to
succeed in its goal, all of its members need to
agree on the goal; understand their role in working
towards it; be trained in how to perform that
role; and have someone providing feedback on
how they are performing, both to correct errors or
inefficiencies, and to allow them to recognise and
feel appreciated for great performance.

Traditional accessibility guidelines have concentrated
almost exclusively on what developers, designers
and content creators (the seven ordinary rowers
in our analogy) need to do to deliver accessibility,

without understanding that their work can be either facilitated or hindered by the layers of more strategic management and policy above them.

Chapter 4 will look at ways of embedding accessibility as a value, goal and competence in *all* the people and policies in your organisation that have an impact on whether your products are made to be accessible.

Enable process

Once you've embedded accessibility as a value within your organisation's staff and policies, the third key is critical to ensure that you are able to deliver it *consistently* for all your products, whether they are similar or vary in purpose, audience, technology or importance. This is about identifying a way of working that is stable enough to ensure good accessibility results every time, while being flexible enough to handle any type of project you throw at it without breaking.

I'm talking about enabling your teams to get accessibility right, and to get it right all of the time. And to be clear, I'm not talking about a *checklist* – something that seems to be synonymous with accessibility in many people's minds; I'm talking about a *process*. A documented, flexible, repeatable process that each member of your project team buys into for every web project your organisation runs.

As establishing a new process or change to your current process into the way you work is much more difficult to achieve than adding a checklist into your quality assurance testing, it's important for me to convince you why this is necessary. On 27 January 2012, the Royal National Institute of Blind People (RNIB) – the UK's leading vision impairment charity – served legal papers on the airline bmibaby for its failure to ensure that blind and partially sighted customers could book flights via its website.[1]

I'd like you to put yourself in bmibaby's shoes for a moment and consider what you would do in this circumstance...

I'm guessing that on the day the legal writ arrived, your web team would already be up to their necks in creating new website features or new ways of beating the competition via sales funnel conversion optimisation; getting the site to work better for people using it on a mobile phone; trying to maximise search engine optimisation (SEO) and Google pay-per-click conversions; making sure that they were monitoring Twitter and Facebook for any mentions of your organisation in the social media sphere, especially detrimental ones; pushing out the online part of marketing campaigns to sell more flights via promotions or link-ups with affiliates' websites. Each one of these to-do list items is designed to maintain or improve your organisation's visibility on the web or improve the conversion of site visitors to customers. And each one of these to-do list items needs the investment of the web team's time and energy to bring in greater revenues and profits for the company.

Into this already busy environment, the notice of legal proceedings would drop like a bombshell. And the only sensible questions to ask in response are: 'What is the minimum we need to do to make the pain go away?' and 'When do we need to do it by?' It's all hands to the pump on 'remediation' – bailing out the water in your boat and plugging the leak so you can get back to the important thing, which is sailing into the new waters already scheduled on your map.

This makes perfect sense, but it is likely to create a problem as well as solve one.

To illustrate, let me tell you the story of Achilles.

As anyone who's seen Brad Pitt's impressive combat prowess in the film *Troy* will be all too aware, Achilles was an incredible Greek warrior whose name struck fear into his opponents. He would doubtless be dismayed to find that he is renowned in modern popular culture for one part of his anatomy only: his heel.[2]

Rather than actually dealing with his one weakness, Achilles did the first century AD equivalent of putting a Band-Aid on it. This dealt with the problem immediately, but it didn't deal with it long term. And so Achilles has gone down in history as a cautionary tale, rather than being celebrated as a mighty warrior.

Why am I bringing ancient Greeks into a book on accessibility? Because fixing the accessibility problems of our website or mobile app when they are pointed out to us by an audit or user complaint is our Achilles' heel. We may want to feel that we've learnt from Achilles' unintended message to us throughout the centuries, but most organisations are treating accessibility just like a Band-Aid. Why else would 'accessibility remediation' still be such a core service from any accessibility agency?

This highlights a direct link with many organisations' limited view of the first key: expand awareness. If we're trying to 'get away with it', we'll only think of accessibility when we get caught, and then we'll rush to find the quickest, cheapest Band-Aid to make the pain go away so we can forget about it again.

The quick, cheap way of dealing with pain is the patch-up pill, not the lifestyle change that prevents the pain coming back. Yet any sensible person knows that prevention is better than cure. The fact is that we need to fix the problem in the *process* not the *product* to prevent it reoccurring.

No website or app is ever finished. Most go through content and maintenance updates every day, minor version updates weekly or monthly, and full rebuilds every couple of years. So fixing your accessibility problem in the product rather than in the way you work means that every time you upgrade your product, you may cause new accessibility problems to occur, especially as experienced product team members move on to new challenges and new team members take their place.

ISO 30071-1's best-practice advice is to enable your staff to get accessibility right all the time by embedding it in your standard digital production process, because then you will uphold accessibility not only in every new product that you create, but also in every version of those products.

While embedding accessibility in your process is more challenging to accomplish than just asking one person to test the product against a checklist and do whatever fixes are necessary, its benefits are much greater. Chapter 5 will provide an overview of the activities to include in your digital production process to consistently enable your teams to prevent accessibility problems coming up in the first place (for the detail, you will need this book's companion: *Inclusive Design for Products*) so pain relief isn't such a necessary part of the picture.

Measure effects

The fourth key is the one most organisations don't think about nearly enough. Often it's only something they appreciate when they think they've done everything they were supposed to do, and yet they are still faced with an email from a person with a disability accusing them of not doing the right thing. Ignoring this key can take an organisation that's done the work to get good at accessibility and turn it into one that slowly decides not to bother any more.

It is measuring the effects your accessibility work achieves. After all, if accessibility is about winning, then it is fundamentally about the effect your work has on the user experience of the disabled people you're trying to help, and the rest of your non-disabled users.

Unfortunately, this often gets forgotten, especially as checking compliance with guidelines is the one thing most people know about accessibility. This is like working out where you've come to at the end of a drive by double-checking all of the turns you made on the way, rather than by looking out of the window and asking a local where you are. You could have taken all the 'right' turns according to the map, but what if the map is a little out of date?

ISO 30071-1 uses technical accessibility standards like WCAG to do what they are good at – providing detailed instructions for how to make decisions on various technical, design and content aspects of accessibility as you create and maintain a product. What it doesn't use WCAG for is what it's not good at – telling you whether or not following those guidelines has resulted in a product that disabled people can actually use to complete the tasks they came to the site to accomplish. For this is often as much about usability and learnability as accessibility.

To highlight the importance of this, let me tell you another story, of how two days in 2008 pushed me to learn which accessibility outcomes are important for users and organisations, and which are not. Let me take you to a radio studio in BBC Broadcasting House during the hot, sticky days of summer.

If you had been sitting next to me at 2.42 one afternoon, you'd have been sitting at a green baize table looking across at the presenter of the BBC's *In Touch* radio show for people who are blind or visually impaired. He's fascinating. So much so that I'm not paying adequate attention to the frustrated voice coming through my headphones. Which is OK until it stops, the red light goes on in front of me and I realise it's my turn to speak.

This is what I'm here for: to defend the accessibility of BBC iPlayer. This shouldn't be a problem. I know we've already done the right thing. And I've prepared notes for my response. Unfortunately, unlike the Braille notes that the programme's presenter has been stroking silently under his arm as a prompt for his flawless introduction, my notes are crisply folded on the green baize in front of me and unfolding them would be likely to create noise that would be picked up by the microphone.

So I speak from the heart.

'We really do care for blind users. We care for all our users. That's why we've found the best guidelines for how to make things work for everyone, and have followed them to the letter. We've tested the product with people with all sorts of disabilities. I even checked it with the JAWS screen reader myself this morning and... '

'So why can I not use it? Why did you have to replace something that worked with something that doesn't?'

It's a bit difficult to argue with a disembodied voice, especially live on radio. Wondering who the complaining voice belongs to, to make them more human, to have a chance of properly empathising with their position, I picture a woman in her late forties, sitting at a computer desk somewhere in middle England with a guide dog by her side. But already I'm figuring that this is a stereotype. I don't know much about her, other than she's obviously not happy. And much of what I've pictured may be completely wrong.

And then suddenly I get a flash of insight, a glimpse into her world. That's what she is actually complaining about – our product team haven't given her a good enough picture of the iPlayer we've created. The way we've designed it hasn't enabled her to understand how to use this thing she cannot see.

I'm really loving this train of thought, this insight into the needs of this user, seeing all sorts of implications for how we could...

The presenter coughs, and suddenly I'm back in the room. These insights are helpful. But they're not answering her question.

'I, er... er... '

He rescues me. 'Thankfully, not all blind users are having the same problem. Here are a number of blind people we spoke to yesterday who say that they love the product...'

The red light turns off as altogether more friendly voices soothe my ears.

The presenter gestures for me to take my headphones off. His words are for me, not our audience.

'Just a word of advice. It's not the work you do, it's whether or not it helps people that matters. Wouldn't you say?'

He's right. I've dodged a bullet as the usability and accessibility of the site – the requirements of my job – seem OK. But even going beyond guidelines and accessibility conformance and doing user testing to check the usability of our site for disabled people hasn't been enough. For this person, the *learnability* of our product is the problem. She had something that worked. We have replaced it with a version two that works in a different way, and we haven't helped her move from one to the other. And it sounds like the blind people we recruited for our testing may have been way more confident and competent in their use of the web than the majority of blind people out there. We may have been ahead of organisations that just do 'compliance'. But in reality, there's still a long way to go in our journey...

As I sit at my desk the next day, my boss places a letter in front of me as he breezes past.

'Sort this out.'

Two sentences of the first paragraph of typed text are underlined in red:

'I was disgusted to hear that you only test your sites using the JAWS screen reader. How exactly do you expect a pensioner to afford £800?'

The name on the bottom of the letter is a man's, so it's certainly not the woman from yesterday. But I have learnt from listening to her. This time I have the opportunity to engage more deeply with this user's real-world difficulties. There is more to be learnt. And this time, in private. I pick up the phone and dial the number at the bottom of the page...

Two weeks later, my team and I launch the UK's first survey into which screen readers blind people are actually using. We've bypassed asking the screen reader manufacturers and their distributors; we're talking directly to a wide variety of blind users, partnering with the RNIB to ask people on their mailing list what sort of user experience they are getting from our websites on the screen readers they use.

The time for assumptions is over: now we are going to arm ourselves with better research on which to make our decisions. And we're going to test with people who actually make up the majority of our disabled audiences, not techies whose vision impairment isn't as key to their user experience as their amazing capability to work around problems.

WCAG? It would only be the end of our journey if we didn't care whether real people were able to use the products resulting from our hard work. As we do, it's just the start.

In summary, I believe the aim of accessibility – or inclusion, as I prefer to call it – is to build a *better* product, not just a *compliant* one. Because through this lies sufficient return on investment (ROI) to make the costs of accessibility worthwhile.

That's the other effect you want to have – a positive impact on your organisation's bottom line – for accessibility to help you achieve your business goals. And a positive ROI is definitely possible.

To give one example of the bottom-line benefits of considering the needs of disabled and older people, take OXO Good Grips – a well-known American pioneer of inclusive design. Sam Farber's wife, a keen cook, suffered from arthritis, which caused her to ask him one challenging but inspiring question: 'Why do ordinary kitchen tools hurt your hands?' The result of him engaging fully with that question and how to answer it made him found OXO[3] and created the company's fortune.

The company's first fifteen products launched in 1990. They achieved sales growth of over 35% per year from 1991 to 2002. OXO's line of kitchen products has now grown to over 500 and the company has won over 100 design awards.

Now that sounds like winning to me!

'Start with the end in mind' is always a useful policy, so Chapter 6 helps you ensure your accessibility strategy keeps this end firmly in mind, and how to measure the impact of your strategy over time to make sure your work is having the effects you want to make it sustainable.

Continually evolve

The fifth key is one that you may think is just for organisations that are already getting good at accessibility and inclusive design. But it includes the one thing that accessibility has to potentially make your organisation rich – innovation. And you don't need to be a tech giant to do it.

It is continually evolving the way you deliver accessibility. If the fourth key allows you to prove that accessibility is worth continually investing in as you can prove it has good ROI, this is about making sure that your investment is reviewed for efficiencies and your return reviewed for opportunities.

Accessibility and inclusion are never 'done'. Technology is constantly changing and improving, so knowing how to evolve your accessibility thinking and practice is essential. What's more, thinking differently can actually help you move technology forwards. Innovation comes with the territory. If you're thinking 'We're good at this already, what's next?' then this is for you.

For inclusion to thrive in an organisation, you need to continually be reviewing the strengths, weakness, opportunities and threats in your current practices to improve the way you do it. What worked last year may not work with the latest updates in devices, operating systems (OSes), technology frameworks or design thinking. And more importantly, real opportunities to differentiate your organisation from your competitors could be hidden in the user research you've done or the accessibility challenges your teams have been facing.

What's more, if you seize those opportunities, you reframe accessibility for teams. From seeing it as a frustrating exercise in following rules that slow down product development, they will view it instead as an exercise in questioning all the established conventions of digital to create something innovative. Accessibility done well can be the sort of thing that helps you retain the best people in your organisation as you use its challenges to spark their creativity, not hinder it.

To highlight the opportunities, let me tell you another story, of how saying yes to an accessibility challenge turned into a constant stream of innovation reaching far beyond the original people it aimed to help.

In 2011, the UK advisory service on technology and inclusion JISC TechDis approached me to judge a contest to investigate how gesture recognition could help learners with disabilities who lack independence due to an inability to communicate by speech or lack of motor control. As I'd done a number of innovation projects with Gamelab UK and Reflex Arc when I was at the BBC, I decided that I didn't want to judge the contest, I wanted to win it for my new company, Hassell Inclusion.

Together, the three companies came up with a proposal for the contest and secured two phases of funding to create a Makaton sign-language recognition system to help autistic and learning-disabled Makaton users make an easier transition into independent living and employment. Hassell Inclusion led the project's user research and product design, working with specialist colleges across the UK, investigating the user contexts in which sign and gesture recognition would be both useful and appropriate for students and older adults who use Makaton. Our user research also identified ways of motivating our target users to use our evolving recognition technologies, resulting in gameplay concepts to engage users with signing in familiar scenarios.

The resulting uKinect sign-language eLearning games enabled these young people, along with their new non-signing colleagues, to learn workplace-specific sign vocabularies to help them transition from college to work environments. The games used an engaging animated avatar called Boris who demonstrated and responded to signs via an innovative Kinect sign-language recognition system. As well as being useful for these learners, the 'Boris Games' also demonstrated what was possible through sign-language recognition and won the TIGA Games Industry Award for Best Education Initiative in 2013.

Through the years, the innovations in response to the needs of these initial groups of people have enabled us to create similar breakthroughs for other groups.

Microsoft, whose Kinect was at the heart of the breakthrough in gesture recognition we created, put us in touch with the Guide Dogs charity that was looking for ways of making mobility training more fun for blind and partially sighted children. Working with a school for vision-impaired kids in

North London, we created the Nepalese Necklace games which took the body- and spatial-awareness exercises the kids had to get good at performing and made them controls for motivational 3D audio-games, turning 'boring' exercises into fun activities. The games transformed the kids' feelings towards their mobility training and improved their concentration on the rest of their schoolwork. They also won our team the Guide Dogs Partner of the Year award.

Microsoft also put us in touch with a hospital in Reading, UK, that had been using Kinect games to help stroke patients' rehabilitation. The use of movement to control games was motivational for the patients, but the games' movements weren't the optimal ones recommended by their therapists and the games took too long to get started. We secured funding from Innovate UK to investigate whether gesture-based games created specifically to motivate stroke patients to repeat key exercises could drive their recovery of function without requiring occupational therapists and physiotherapists to constantly be present to guide and motivate them.

Over the course of the next six months we proved that we could do this, freeing up therapists to concentrate on higher levels of care for their patients, making more effective use of their valuable time. Our project was voted best presentation in its category at the Collaboration Nation event showcasing all projects Innovate UK funded in 2014.

Since then, Gamelab and Reflex Arc have taken the results of this innovation further into rehabilitation, adding virtual reality (VR) components and beyond.

As Richard England, Reflex Arc's CEO, says:

'When we started working with Hassell Inclusion to help students with communication difficulties, I never thought it would give me experience and skills that would help me create innovative mainstream VR experiences for the likes of Reebok. This is where thinking differently has got us. It's been quite some journey...'

This is just one example of a thriving sector of startups betting on innovation prompted by the needs of people with disabilities. Accessibility innovation is not just for the tech giants; it's for anyone with the imagination to make it happen. Chapter 7 will give you inspiration and pointers to take your journey to the next level.

ISO 30071-1: your shortcut to accessibility maturity

'Do you want to avoid losing? Or do you want to win?'

'Embed it so that, like a stick of seaside rock, you can take a cross section of any aspect of your organisation and find the same values at play.'

'You need to fix the problem in the process not the product to prevent it reoccurring.'

'It's not the work you do; it's whether or not it helps people that matters.'

'This is where thinking differently has got us.'

These are the phrases that have steered me and my usability and accessibility team at the BBC, and then my team at Hassell Inclusion, all through the years since that radio show in 2008.

Three years later, we had begun to put in place many of the things necessary to make sure our hard work at the BBC was really getting through to our users. More importantly, the British Standards Institution had given me a chance to take that experience, enrich it by comparing it against what the heads of accessibility in other best-practice organisations had done, and create BS 8878 to show others how they could do the same thing, and maybe win the awards we had won, providing organisational and process guidance to go with the technical requirements in WCAG. And eight years later, ISO has given me the chance to look at BS 8878 from the perspectives of experts in Austria, Canada, China, France, Germany, Holland, Japan, Korea, Spain, Sweden and the USA to deliver ISO 30071-1.

ISO 30071-1 is built on the combined experience of some of the world's most able accessibility experts – from those on my IST/45 committee at BSI, to those on international committee ISO/IEC JTC 1, Information technology, Subcommittee SC 35, User interfaces at ISO. It captures the progress in the accessibility journeys they've made so you can take a shortcut.

While BS 8878 provided advice on how to create or procure accessible websites and mobile apps, ISO 30071-1 extends this to digital products (or ICT systems, to use the language in the standard) used on a wider set of devices, including VR/augmented reality (AR) headsets, smart speakers, kiosks, in-flight and in-car entertainment systems, games consoles, ATMs and electronic point of sales systems. It also considers the context of use of these products and what to do when the assistive technologies and accessibility guidelines that usually enable digital products to be accessible are not available on a device.

ISO 30071-1 has taken BS 8878's sixteen-step process for ensuring digital products are accessible when launched and maintained, and streamlined it into eight activities that can be integrated with whatever software development lifecycle methodology teams are using to create their products. ISO 30071-1 updates and clarifies BS 8878's advice on the relationship between inclusive design and user-personalised approaches to accessibility, including when to consider providing additional personalised accessibility provisions. It also updates the advice on business cases in BS 8878 to make it more appropriate for legislation and regulations in different countries which encourage or mandate accessibility.

It was launched in May 2019.

What digital products, hybrid products and ICT systems does ISO 30071-1 cover?

BS 8878 used the term 'web product' to denote the product being created. This was to make sure that people were aware that the standard applied:

- To different product types:

  - Intranet and extranet websites and workplace applications for staff, as well as external internet websites

  - 'Software as a service' cloud services (eg Google Docs), rich internet applications (eg Netflix), online games platforms (eg Club Penguin Online) as well as static information sites

  - Sites where content is created by users (eg social media, blogs and online encyclopaedias) as well as sites where content is created by the site owner (eg company information sites)

- On different delivery platforms and technologies:

  - Mobile websites and apps, as well as desktop websites

In ISO 30071-1 we extended the scope of the digital products the standard applies to, as our experience of using BS 8878 had indicated that its approach and harmonisation with non-digital inclusive design processes made it appropriate to extend to wider ICT systems and hybrid systems, such as:

- Social media

- Virtual assistants and chatbots

- VR/AR apps, and apps for smart speakers and kiosks

- Games on games consoles

- Apps for in-flight and in-car entertainment systems

- Software in ATMs and electronic point of sales systems

- ICT used in internet of things and smart cities

I've even used it to help an advertising agency think about the accessibility of motor show stands.

ISO 30071-1 uses the term 'ICT systems' to encompass this wider scope. But in this book, to ease understanding I'm going to use the more familiar term 'digital products'.

How this book expands on ISO 30071-1

This book is a guide to what's in ISO 30071-1 and includes the experience of my team at Hassell Inclusion of user testing its value (and BS 8878's before it) in the real world of digital product creation, not only in the UK but also internationally.

We've trained over fifty organisations in using BS 8878 to set their accessibility strategy in the nine years since its publication, and many of our insights from this experience have improved ISO 30071-1 to ensure it reflects the reality of digital production in 2019. We've also created tools and captured real-world examples to help people implement the standards in the culture of their organisation.

To illustrate many of the book's points and add real-world depth, I've included quotes from interviews I've conducted with some of the world's top accessibility minds on their areas of greatest expertise:

• Members of my team of experts at Hassell Inclusion on how people learn accessibility

• A United Nations (UN) agency director on how accessibility laws are created

- Experts on understanding disabled and older people's use of digital products

- Experts in how to commission and carry out accessibility testing

- The creator of the accessibility ecosystem in Qatar

- People who've embedded accessibility in a multinational IT company, a Canadian bank, the American State of Texas, the Australian government, university document repositories and innovative eLearning games

In the support materials for this book, there are many such interviews, so I'd encourage you to register for them now to delve deeper into anything that particularly resonates with you as you make your journey.

I know that ISO 30071-1 can get you from the pain of confusion about accessibility to award-winning results because it's an expression of the journey that I, and many other accessibility experts, have gone on before you.

So let's dive in!

THREE

Expand Awareness – Why Bother?

There are a number of reasons why an organisation might be interested in supporting the needs of people with disabilities and older audiences (ISO 30071-1 calls these diverse users). Different organisations may have different reasons at play behind their strategy.

Are they in it because of choice or necessity, for risk aversion, to keep up good corporate social responsibility, to maximise their products' audience reach or a combination of these? And how important are each of these to the organisation in comparison to the others?

There can often be a real difference between the public communication of these reasons and what the organisation communicates internally to its digital production staff. Organisations are often required to hold a particular position by their public service nature or sheer size and publish laudable words about their commitment to accessibility publicly, but the *reality* is many organisations' commitment to inclusion and accessibility often doesn't live up to their fine words as their staff aren't trained to live out the commitment and projects fail to prioritise it consistently. These organisations need to decide how important inclusion is in comparison to other priorities, to avoid 'flip-flopping' between reasons for doing accessibility depending on the situation in front of them.

This chapter will help you work out what your motivation is for inclusion and what the goals of your accessibility strategy will be: avoiding being sued; minimising the costs of dealing with accessibility complaints; becoming 'best practice'; ensuring you're not missing a sales feature compared with your competitors; selling more products; gaining more customers. This is an essential foundation as you can only build a strategic framework for *how* you are going to embed accessibility in your organisation if you know the reasons *why* you are doing it and its relative priority to other strategies you're also pursuing.

Meet your disabled and older audiences

Let's start off by getting a better idea of the disabled and older audiences whose access needs come under the heading of accessibility.

In most Western countries the size of the disabled population ranges between 12% and 26% of the overall population. To give a couple of examples: in the UK, that's almost 14 million people; in Brazil, it's over 24 million people. In the Asia-Pacific region there are 690 million people with disabilities whose unmet needs and rights were brought to the attention of local governments and brands by the 2018 Asian Para Games.[1]

These are big numbers.

Many digital professionals are initially puzzled or even sceptical about these large numbers. How can there be 20% of the population who are disabled if you don't see them every day on the street? What does disability actually mean in the context of audience size? Who is defined as disabled? What's interesting is that when you go deeper to answer these questions, you often find that the numbers tend to *under*-estimate the prevalence of disability.

INCLUSIVE DESIGN FOR ORGANISATIONS

Here in the UK, disability is defined by the Equality
Act 2010[2] as:

> '...anyone with a physical or mental
> impairment which has a substantial long-term
> adverse effect on their ability to carry out
> normal day-to-day activities'.

This includes people with mental-health issues or
people with a long-term illness that impacts their
day-to-day life, but it doesn't include anybody
who wouldn't consider themselves disabled or
wouldn't be comfortable disclosing their disability
to a census. So people who are dyslexic are likely to
be underrepresented in these figures because many
dyslexics unfortunately regard their condition as
'their guilty secret', not something that they would
wish to disclose.

While the number of people with disabilities who
are not comfortable making such a disclosure tends
to underplay these figures here in the UK, it is even
more notable in parts of the world where disability
is unfortunately still seen as something to be hidden,
either by the person with the disability themselves or
their immediate family.

One other thing that tends to shock people who
attend Hassell Inclusion's workshops is the slide

on how the disabled population breaks down into different disability groups. You probably know that it's important to make sure that your website works well for blind people using screen readers because they may sue you if it doesn't. And yet the proportion of blind people in the disabled population is approximately 2%, so making your website work for blind people alone may devote all your time and attention to 2% of your potential audience and neglect the needs of the other 98%, which includes many more people with lower-level vision impairments.

That makes no sense from anything other than a risk-avoidance perspective.

This bias towards considering the needs of people with more extreme disabilities is not confined to vision impairment. The larger groups of disabled people are those with more minor impairments, and yet we tend to concentrate on the extremes because their need is greatest and their lobbies are strongest.

For a fuller discussion on the impact of these issues on the prioritisation of solutions for people with different disabilities, see the section on ISO 30071-1's Activity 1 in this book's companion, *Inclusive Design for Products*.

Older people

One further group that is impacted by accessibility issues is the ageing population.

Most websites and apps are created by young people. But the services that they provide may potentially appeal to older people as much as those who are younger. As 'baby boomers outspend every other generation by $400 billion annually, providing over 50 percent of U.S. consumption',[3] it could be that they are your most important, underserved audience.

As many people develop impairments through the ageing process, we should all be interested in how these people are supported by digital products. In the future, 'they' will become 'we'. It's not something we necessarily like to think about, but we will all develop impairments in time. So, we all have something to gain from designing for our future selves.

On top of this, the statistics on population ageing are startling. At present about 18% of the UK's population are likely to have a combination of access needs due to ageing rather than disability.[4] Every month more than a quarter of a million Americans turn sixty-five[5] and the population forecasts

from Japan for 2050 predict a massive ongoing
demographic change:

- In 1950, over sixty-five-year-olds made up 4.9%
  of the population

- By 2012, this percentage had risen to 24.1%

- Projections for 2050 indicate this figure will reach
  almost 39%

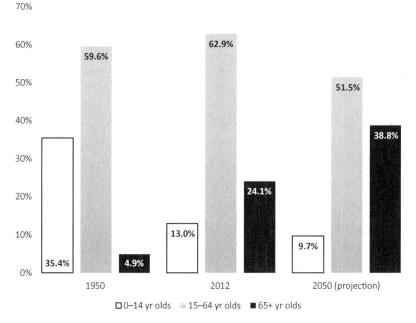

*The impact of population ageing: changes in the population of Japan
(Source: Japan Statistics Bureau, MIC, Ministry of Health, Labour and Welfare)*

This is one of the reasons why accessibility is so important economically in Japan and why the country needed ISO 30071-1 to be created to deliver it.

On top of the pensions 'time bomb' is the increasing need for people to be able to continue living independently in their homes as they age. The gross domestic product (GDP) of a nation like Japan will nosedive if 40% of the population can no longer use digital technologies in their seventies and eighties and will require those in the working population to spend their time helping them counter digital exclusion.

Similarly, from your organisation's perspective, it is clear that if accessibility is important today, it will only get more important over the coming years as the number of people with impairments in the population who wish to use your digital products grows. While you may be able to exclude older people from using your website without too much loss to your bottom line at the moment, year on year this decision will start to cost you more and more. I congratulate you on having purchased this book now and started on your journey of understanding the access needs of people with impairments. The insights you'll get from taking inclusion seriously will only become more valuable as time goes on. Act now, and over time your foresight could turn into a great advantage over your competitors who came late to the party.

Here's what Makoto Ueki, Accessibility Consultant at Infoaxia and Chair of Japan's Web Accessibility Infrastructure Committee, said when I interviewed him:

> 'Japan is the world's fastest ageing country. As we are ageing, many more people will think about accessibility as "My issue. It's needed for me. My daily life heavily relies on the web. If I can't use the web, I will get lost. No web, no life." And accessibility is not just about people with disabilities and elderly people; it's about everybody. The web will be accessed by many more kinds of devices, environments, and it's going to be diverse.'

Let's look at all the reasons why the needs of disabled and older people should matter to your organisation now. We'll look at both organisational threats and opportunities.

Threat – the legal business case

The first threat is well known to most website owners as it's the one that disabled people and accessibility advocates have used most frequently in fighting for their needs to be taken into account when digital technologies are created.

It's the legal threat.

Most countries have some form of anti-discrimination legislation on their statute books. In the UK it's the Equality Act 2010. In the United States it's the Americans with Disabilities Act of 1990 (ADA),[6] together with a number of state laws. Regulations implementing the EU Directive on Web Accessibility require public sector websites and mobile applications to achieve WCAG 2.1 by September 2020 at the latest.[7]

And those countries that haven't yet established disability discrimination legislation are likely to soon. The UN Convention on the Rights of Persons with Disabilities[8] – which now has signatories from over 161 nation states worldwide – is the driving force behind much of the creation of this legislation. Countries that sign the convention commit to starting on the path towards creating disability

discrimination legislation, usually establishing it
within the next ten years.

While the strength and wording of these laws
differ, the purpose of most is to clearly establish
that disabled people may have grounds for making
a discrimination claim against the owners of a
product or service if that service has not been
made available and usable for them. Most of these
disability discrimination laws apply to products
and services provided through websites and mobile
apps, either mentioned explicitly in the legislation
(as in the Australian Disability Discrimination
Act 1992[9]) or as case law establishes that websites
should be considered to be services like those
traditionally offered through physical premises or
phone lines (as was arguably established for the
ADA by a ruling in the US National Association of
the Deaf vs Netflix suit in 2012[10]). In most cases a
principle of 'reasonableness'[11] is included in the
law, to differentiate between the clear need for large,
important online services (such as government
services or banks) to be made accessible and the
lesser need for smaller, less popular websites (such
as personal blogs) to be made accessible.

To complicate matters, disability discrimination law
in some countries, like the UK and the USA, applies
to both publicly and privately owned websites, but

in others like France[12] it only applies to publicly owned sites. The W3C Web Access Initiative (WAI) Web Accessibility Laws & Policies site[13] is a good source of information to find out what is in force in your country.

On top of general disability discrimination law, some countries have also passed specific accessibility legislation for different industries which impacts on their online presence. Two examples, both from the USA, are:

- The 21st Century Video Accessibility Act of 2010 (CVAA),[14] which includes requirements that full-length programmes and clips[15] that have been broadcast with captions on TV are also closed captioned when they are made available on the internet

- The amendment to the Air Carrier Access Act of 1986 (ACAA),[16] in which the United States Department of Transportation has taken steps to address the accessibility of air carrier websites and kiosks to persons with disabilities

While some of these laws have been in existence for decades, the amount of case law linked to them varies from country to country. To give a few examples:

- In the UK there is no case law for web accessibility. Even though Part III of the Disability Discrimination Act[17] – which protected the rights of disabled people before the Equality Act – came into being at the end of the 1990s, no cases have come to UK court for ruling. All the cases that have been brought have been settled out of court, thus depriving organisations from the clarity of application information that comes from published rulings.

- In the United States, the number of accessibility lawsuits grows steadily each year, with 2,285 lawsuits in 2018, up 181% over 2017.[18] High-profile cases like the National Federation of the Blind vs Target case,[19] well known for its $6 million settlement in 2008, provide an indication of how courts in the different states might rule on new cases presented to them.

- In Australia, case law stretches back to Maguire vs Sydney Organising Committee for the Olympic Games (SOCOG)[20] around the Sydney Olympics in 2000, which was the first case for web accessibility globally.

The legal situation in many countries is constantly changing, so organisations should keep themselves informed on legislation and cases in all of the jurisdictions in which their websites and apps are available. You can keep up to date with the latest laws and key cases in Lainey Feingold's great legal updates.[21]

While disability discrimination laws help raise awareness of the access needs of disabled people, organisations that are motivated purely because of the legal business case for accessibility tend to see it as a 'necessary cost' of doing business online, like data protection or website security. As such, they naturally wish to spend as little on it as possible, for it is an insurance policy that they are not convinced they need. Even the most stringent accessibility laws – like the Accessibility for Ontarians with Disabilities Act 2010 (AODA) – aren't effective without enforcement.[22]

This perspective makes perfect sense as it's similar to how I buy my insurance, whether for my house or car. While I know insurance is a condition of my mortgage and my ability to remain legal on the road, and while I know that it is possible that I *may* need to claim at some point, when I *buy* my insurance I go to a price comparison website and generally find the cheapest insurance available, because *at that point* I'm more interested in the cost than the benefits of the policies on offer.

As Debra Ruh, CEO and Founder of Ruh Global Impact, USA, put it when I interviewed her:

'The reality in the United States is that large corporations get sued all the time – we are a very litigious society. We put our laws on books and then we pound our laws out by suing each other. It's become very fear based, "You'd better be compliant, you'd better be accessible or the community of people with disabilities are going to get you." It's a sort of "Who wants to be a millionaire? Let me pick which corporation I'm going to sue." But the problem with the fear-based approach is that it creates an "us against them" thing, and people don't change behaviours because of fear. Or if they do, it'll be temporary.'

As the large numbers of cases and settlements in the USA show, the costs of being the target for litigation are real. However, people with disabilities who bring cases want organisations to change their behaviour, not get fined. Lainey Feingold, a US disability rights lawyer who works primarily with the blind and visually impaired community, talked about this when I interviewed her:

'In 1995 we wrote to three banks in California and said, "Your ATMs don't work for blind people. Rather than us filing a lawsuit, will you be willing to work with us?" In 1999 we got our first agreement on talking ATMs.

Since then we've done forty-nine agreements, and we got into web as web became bigger, and now into mobile.

'There are challenges inside these corporations to get the right thing done. Settlements generally require companies to hire somebody to be responsible for accessibility, reporting to the chief information officer. They have to train their staff. They have to get people in to audit accessibility. They have to make sure that they embed it in their processes. As we help make that easier by not bringing in a bunch of suits to fight, I think that's why we've been successful.'

Threat – the regulatory business case

In some countries there are regulations that place obligations on public organisations to promote equality of opportunity between disabled and non-disabled people when carrying out their functions. In the UK, for example, the Public Sector Equality Duty[23] requires public organisations to create their own Single Equality Scheme (which replaced the previous Disabled Equality Scheme) to explain how they will do this across all of their areas of responsibility, including their digital communications, and to publish the scheme publicly.

Statements of accessibility policy are also becoming more common elsewhere. The Canadian Province of Ontario's AODA requires all businesses to create an accessibility policy,[24] and there are moves towards states in the USA requiring the companies from which they procure digital products to include these policies, for example the Policy Driven Adoption for Accessibility (PDAA) pilot in the State of Texas.[25]

Any regulation that requires policies to be drafted and published by organisations needs a deeper level of thought and engagement with accessibility than anti-discrimination laws. My team's anecdotal evidence in the UK and Jeff Kline's in the USA has found that these 'policy-based approaches' can be very effective in motivating organisations to get serious about accessibility.[26]

Threat and opportunity – the ethical business case

The second business case for accessibility is the ethical business case. The basis of this case is the assertion that it is unethical or contrary to human-rights to unnecessarily exclude disabled people from the benefits of modern digital technologies that increase their ability to live independently and be fully engaged members of society.

I'll illustrate this with a story.

A few years ago, I was invited back to my alma mater – the University of York in northern England – to present a lecture to the Human-Computer Interaction Group that I used to be part of when researching for my doctorate in the early 1990s. After the lecture, one of the researchers asked if he could buy me coffee later that afternoon to discuss some research that he had done into how well WCAG 2.0 – the international standards for accessibility – predicted the accessibility difficulties disabled people would have with a website.[27] We agreed to meet in two hours in the department coffee shop.

I went to the coffee shop to catch up on the latest progress of some of my projects. But when I asked if the café had wi-fi, I was told that it was only available to students and delegates attending conferences.

No problem, I thought, I'll just use 3G and tether my phone to my Mac so I can work as normal. However, the location of the department was such that not only did I not have any 3G coverage, but I also didn't have 2G or even 1G. As I had not taken the mobile phone number of the researcher, there was no way I could let him know that I needed to meet him in a place with internet coverage, so I stayed in the coffee shop for two hours with no internet.

When was the last time you became acutely aware of the level of dependence that you have on being online? This was mine. My dependence on the internet is encouraged by all of the cloud services I regularly use to run both my business and personal life. Everything, from the way I listen to music using Spotify, to the way I communicate with my family via text and online messaging, to the way I collaborate on projects that I manage via Dropbox and Google Docs, to the way I run my agenda via iCloud, to the way I know where I am and where I need to get to via Google Maps, either works better with an internet connection, or absolutely demands one.

Granted, I didn't have most of these services constantly available to me until the last ten years, but now I've started using them, I am both facilitated and made efficient by them, which has made me dependent on them. They've become the way I work. And on that particular afternoon the support they give me was not available, which made me uncomfortable, disempowered and bored.

What was worse, all around me students were lounging with their laptops and full access to all the online services they could want. Because they were forbidden to give me the wi-fi password, and because there was no way I could think of to get it for myself by any other means, I was excluded from all the benefits modern technology brings. Everyone around me was living the great digital technology dream. And, for a while at least, I wasn't allowed into the club.

Have you ever been in that situation?

The difference between my situation and that of many disabled people is that my situation was temporary and brought about by my own choices, whereas digital exclusion for disabled people is usually permanent or fluctuating, and brought about by the choices of the owners of the websites and apps that they are locked out of. My two hours of boredom was just the merest glimpse into the regular frustrations that many disabled people experience in trying to use modern digital technologies. No wonder that many decide not to bother, unless they have no other choice.

But if they do opt out, they are missing out on real benefits. Reports such as the Digital Britain Report

2009[28] document many of the benefits of being online, from being able to access cheaper products and services using price comparison websites, to accessing cheaper phone calls using services like Skype. Moreover, many organisations are increasingly encouraging their customers to interact with them online, as the savings that they can get from moving existing call-centre or high-street services online can be massive, whether they're passed on to customers through 'online only' deals or not. In the UK, as in many other countries, this move of services online may be one of the ways that a government can streamline itself and provide a more financially efficient service to its population. Private companies can create more shareholder benefits using the same strategy and maximise the value of their customer care budgets.

But this depends on *all* citizens and customers being able to access and use online services. The march to make all services 'digital by default', to use the UK government's term, is only going to become more prevalent, and so the ethical business case that such online services must be accessible will become more compelling as time goes on.

Most organisations feel the potential threat from this ethical case when it comes to brand value. While they may not be aware of all the aspects of the ethical business case for accessibility, most citizens are convinced by it almost instinctively, and so when they hear of the case of an organisation not allowing a disabled person to book a seat on a plane using the operator's website (as was the case in the RNIB vs bmibaby case) or accusations that Beyoncé's Parkwood Entertainment website is not accessible,[29] their opinion of those organisations takes a battering. Whether or not the organisation wins or loses the legal case, in court or behind closed doors, the brand damage has already been done.

I'd argue that, in terms of brand value at least, once the press release has been written by the lawyers representing the disabled complainant, the organisation being sued has already lost.

Of course, promoting the steps your organisation is taking to make your products accessible to disabled people can also be a brand *win*, such as Microsoft enjoyed with the great response to the launch of its Xbox Adaptive Controller.[30]

In the age of corporate social responsibility, large organisations are already aware of the benefits. Making usability and accessibility strategic business objectives is one of the seven principles of being a human-centred organisation (according to ISO 27500), and is part of social responsibility (ISO 26000) and sustainable procurement (ISO 20400). You only have to look at Apple[31] as one example of this, or the public accessibility policies or statements many organisations publish on their websites stating their commitment to accessibility.[32]

While public organisations in the UK are required to do this, even outside the public sector you can find voluntary statements saying things like:

> 'Our approach is to continue to involve disabled people in our work to highlight the barriers experienced by a diverse range of disabled people, and for disabled people to assist us in identifying how to effectively remove those barriers.'

These statements are laudable, but publishing them without becoming competent in how to live up to them could be a real own goal.

Opportunity – the commercial business case – reach

The next opportunity for most organisations that create websites or mobile apps is that making them accessible can increase the size of their user base, or reach.

If 20% of the population of most countries are disabled, and many more are older or have low literacy, making your digital products accessible is a sensible way of ensuring that as many potential users can use your website as possible. Figures for the 'Purple Pound' – the spending power of disabled people (£249 billion in the UK,[33] $220 billion in the USA[34]) are significant. While these figures could be backed up with stronger research evidence on how improving accessibility can attract this spend to organisations, it surely makes sense to avoid excluding at least 20% of your potential customers from doing business with you.

Moreover, research has found that people with disabilities, and their families and friends, tend to be more loyal to the websites that they've taken the time to become familiar with, rather than jumping to competitors when they win on price comparison, as Axel Leblois, President and Executive Director at G3ict – The Global Initiative for Inclusive ICTs – said when I interviewed him:

> 'Accessibility is the best loyalty programme you can have, more effective than any mileage card, any loyalty card, anything. Japan has really shown the way. They have some mobile phone service providers who have done incredible work to create "best in market"

products for persons with disabilities and seniors, and had tremendous success in gaining new business.'

And, of course, there are well-known site maintenance and SEO benefits to making your web content accessible.[35] Using the right semantic heading tags, writing descriptive alt-text for images and including captions for videos all help your content be more completely indexed by what could be considered the 'biggest blind users in the world' – Google and all other search engines.[36]

We'll come back to this essential aspect of accessibility – and how to measure the reach impact of the accessibility you decide to invest in – in Chapter 6.

Opportunity – the commercial business case – selling tools to clients

If your organisation creates browser-based tools or 'software as a service' apps that you sell to clients, then it's important for you to be aware that increasing numbers of those clients, especially those in the public service, may ask you to prove that your web applications are accessible or can be used to create accessible digital products.

The lack of proven accessibility in your products may prevent you from being considered as a supplier to government organisations in the USA and Europe. The American federal government Section 508 was refreshed in 2018 to align with WCAG 2.0 AA,[37] as were the equivalent accessibility requirements for public procurement of ICT products and services in Europe's EN 301 549.[38] These are now clear – no proof of accessibility (for example an Accessibility Conformance Report based on the Voluntary Product Accessibility Template® [VPAT]),[39] no sale.

Outside the public sector, accessibility could still be a contributory USP to win you a tender, especially where clients indicate accessibility requirements in their invitation to tender (ITT) or request for proposal (RFP) documentation. ISO 30071-1 has been designed to support project teams who are *procuring* digital products, as well as teams *building* them. At Hassell Inclusion, we are regularly called on to help our clients embed accessibility requirements into their standard procurement documentation, and anecdotal evidence indicates BS 8878 has had a wide impact on the presence and quality of the specification of accessibility requirements in procurement documentation.[40] We hope ISO 30071-1 has the same effect internationally.

So gaining proof of your products' accessibility and knowing how to sell that to your clients may be as important an investment to your organisation as any other essential part of your tool's functionality or sales pitch.

Opportunity – the commercial business case – minimising complaints

Another huge opportunity in the commercial business case for accessibility is the ability to minimise complaints from disabled customers.

Often Hassell Inclusion clients tell me they have incurred huge resource costs in dealing with complaints when they have launched internal or external digital products without making sure that they were accessible. Often whole months of product management, business analysis and legal resource can be spent on dealing with the complaint of one disabled person. And in this age of consumer complaints via Twitter and Facebook, the cost to your brand of dealing with complaints unprofessionally in public can be significant, so all complaints have to be carefully handled. What's worse is that during this time, product managers may take their eyes off the great majority of their audience to concentrate on the small number who complain.

As anyone who buys a printer can tell you, it's not the original cost of the printer that matters, it's the ongoing cost of the consumables on top of that initial cost – the 'total cost of ownership'. The same is true of accessibility. Some money spent on making a digital product accessible during its development can save you lots of money once it's launched in terms of minimising complaints and the lower costs of building in accessibility rather than retro-fitting it in response to customer feedback. And the benefits here even apply if you have considered accessibility properly when developing your product, but haven't been able to deliver an accessible user experience for all disabled users for some reason.

In the section on ISO 30071-1's Activity 7 in this book's companion, *Inclusive Design for Products*, I discuss how to communicate what accessibility you have and haven't been able to deliver in such a way as to minimise business risk and pre-empt and channel any accessibility complaints so you can deal with them in an efficient and effective way. I also look at a few cases of what can happen if you don't get that communication right.

Opportunity – the commercial business case – creativity and innovation

The final opportunity in the commercial business case is one that is rarely communicated – encouraging your product team to support real audience diversity makes them *more,* not *less* creative.

Innovation is the lifeblood of most companies; all of the companies my team has worked with are trying to make innovative products that their competitors don't have. And we've found that challenging them to think inclusively can be really helpful.

Our experience is that product teams can initially be a little intimidated when they are asked to design products for people with disabilities. Yet when we've been able to get them past that to thinking of the different needs that people have, they tend to change the way they think about technology. And that makes them more innovative.

If you're stuck in a way of thinking about your product, which is probably similar to that of all your competitors, when someone comes in with a challenging question – for example, 'How would that work for someone who can't see or can't read?' – you have to start thinking differently as you can't just get away with the usual step-by-step iterations.

In ideation circles, this is called 'getting over design fixation'.[41] In general, what people who invent new products find is that everyone, all over the world, including all of their competitors, comes up with the same initial seven ideas for the next version of a product. It's so difficult to get out of the fixation with what already exists that they make one step in each direction, but don't really get anywhere.

The usual practice for getting over fixation at this point would be to do something like drop everything for five minutes and draw an alien – anything to get the team thinking differently. That works, but I find the real-world challenge of designing for people with different needs from your own can work even better.

I once did some brainstorming with a major electrical company in Germany that makes white goods – fridges, that sort of thing. We were looking at ovens, and I said, 'How about this for getting past fixation? I want you to come up with an oven that would support the needs of someone who's older, who can't physically hold up the thing they are trying to put into the oven – the casserole dish or whatever – because they just don't have the strength in their arms.'

One question, and suddenly the team members were in a completely different space in terms of their imagination. And what they came up with, pretty quickly afterwards, was the idea of an oven that was actually in the work surface. The cook pressed a button, and the oven rose up until the shelf that they wanted to put things on to was at the right level. Then the older person could slide the dish from the work surface on to the shelf, press a button and the oven would go down until everything was cooked, at which time it would rise up again and they'd be able to slide the dish out.

Whether or not that could get to market, it was one of the most innovative ideas they'd ever had for what to do next for an oven. It wasn't 'lowest common denominator'; it was an idea worthy of their concept kitchen.

That's how taking challenges from a wider community can lead to better products for everyone. I firmly believe that some of the next big innovations in technology could come from people using this sort of thinking. Why? Because many of the products we take for granted these days were originally created specifically for disabled people.

The first typewriter proven to have worked was built by the Italian, Pellegrino Turri, around 1808 for his blind friend, Countess Carolina Fantoni da Fivizzano, to solve the problem of how she was going to be able

to write.[42] This innovative solution to a problem
'no one else had' has now changed the world, with
typewriter keyboards appearing on everything from
tablet computers to TV screens to interactive kiosks.

Alexander Graham Bell was partly trying to help
people with hearing impairments when he invented
the telephone.[43] Ray Kurzweil – now Google's Chief
Engineer – was trying to help people with a visual
impairment to access books more easily when he
came up with the first 'omni font' optical character
recognition and text-to-speech synthesisers for print-
to-speech reading in 1975.[44]

Closer to the web, back in 2005 I was tasked with
creating an online game to help blind children
improve their maths skills through play. My research
found that few five-year-olds in the UK can master
the complexity of the screen readers that many
blind adults use (mastering elementary maths, in
comparison, is easy). And playing a game purely
through the synthesised speech of screen readers
didn't exactly sound exciting. So my team came
up with three-dimensional audio-games that kids
could play purely using the keyboard and their ears,
inspired by the games blind people were creating for
themselves.

Fast forward to 2012 and mobile games like *Zombies Run!*[45] were using the same innovative audio technologies and audio-gameplay ideas to help motivate people to exercise.

How do you make jogging interesting? Well, the guys behind *Zombies Run!* came up with the idea that you're being chased by zombies. How's that for motivation? They wanted to make sure that the experience – the narrative experience of being chased by zombies – was available to you when you were jogging.

But there's a problem with the idea, because you really shouldn't be looking at a screen when you're jogging. If you do, you're not jogging for that much longer. You're bumping into people around you, falling into holes... To all intents and purposes, when you are jogging, you are 'situationally blind' with respect to the screen on your phone. So the game creators couldn't just put zombies on the screen.

They thought about what people do when they're jogging, which is put their ear-buds in to keep them going via their favourite tunes. And they asked, 'Why not do this via sound?' Effectively the game's output is sound going into your ears: if you're not jogging fast enough, the zombies sound like they're getting close and you might get eaten. And the game's input is what you are doing with your body; where you are in terms of your 'GPS'. The rest is narrative and atmosphere.

That's one example of somebody taking something that came out of the blind audio-games community and finding that it is the solution to a mainstream need. And fundamentally, it was so innovative and fresh that lots of people fell in love with it.

While it's likely that you're not making ovens, typewriters, phones or jogging apps, the same innovation principles apply for the creation of any website or app. Why not use my CSUN-14 SlideShare 'Accessibility and Innovation'[46] to inspire you to think more deeply about your wider audience's needs? And see what innovative ideas arrive...

We'll come back to this essential aspect of accessibility in Chapter 7.

Keeping up with the competition

When presented with these business cases, many organisational leaders have one final question before they arrive at a sensible position on accessibility:

What are our competitors doing?

While this question is reasonable – benchmarking
your policies and product decisions against those
of your competitors is a sensible thing to do for
any organisation – the frequent problem with
applying this logic to digital accessibility is that
most organisations are necessarily private about
the lengths they are going to, to take accessibility
into account. Many more organisations have been
using BS 8878 to help them set their accessibility
strategy than say so in public – publishing vague
commitments on their website seems sufficient to
ward off accusations of negligence.

If an organisation includes an accessibility
conformance badge on its website, that seems like
further evidence that its commitment is actually
impacting its products, but in reality, these badges –
even Accessibility Conformance Reports based on
VPAT – are a poor indicator of accessibility in the
long term.

It is relatively expensive to benchmark the
accessibility of a competitor's products as it requires
some form of accessibility testing, let alone gain
an understanding of the process behind how they
deliver them (which we will discuss in Chapter 5).
Nonetheless, it's worth at least checking to see if

your competitors are showing visible signs of pulling ahead in the accessibility race. Even then, putting off making an investment decision until you see those signs may cost you as it may take a while for investment in accessibility to show visible effects. By the time you notice, you may be way behind your competitors.

NOW IT'S YOUR TURN

- Discuss and agree, at the highest appropriate level of your organisation, which combination of the accessibility business cases presented in this chapter are the most aligned to your organisation's values and priorities. The accessibility strategies of most mature organisations draw from all of the business cases to ensure they don't miss out on gaining the best return from their accessibility investment. If you miss considering any of the cases, you risk undervaluing accessibility to your business. Accessibility is so much more than legal risk insurance.

- To help you facilitate this discussion, listen to Hassell Inclusion's ROI podcast[47] and use the ROI Scorecard in this book's support materials (see Chapter 1) to quickly and easily generate a compelling and informative document detailing the business cases that are appropriate to an organisation of your size, ownership and field of business in your nation.

- Will your organisation aim to be a leader or a follower in accessibility? How should accessibility be balanced with your other organisational and project priorities and audiences? Consider getting an accessibility company to come in to do a value of inclusion workshop – a bespoke presentation on the benefits of accessibility – followed by a strategy workshop to align those benefits with your organisation's business goals.

- Once you've made these decisions, you'll need somewhere to write them down so you can base your decisions on them later in the book, or revisit them if further investigation prompts you to. ISO 30071-1 advises you to do this in a document called an organisational ICT accessibility policy. I'd suggest you download the organisational ICT accessibility policy template in this book's support materials. This is designed to lead you through your considerations to capture your decisions and the reasoning behind them.

FOUR

Embed Strategy – How To Embed Accessibility In Your Organisation

N ow you've got your motivation for doing accessibility agreed, it's important to work out how to do it right in your organisation, and how to do it right all of the time.

If organisations want to embed inclusion into their culture and business-as-usual processes, the accessibility world's solutions unfortunately seem piecemeal and tactical, not strategic. Accessibility is portrayed as something complex, which requires continual advice, even dependency on expert accessibility specialists often from external suppliers.

While it is true that accessibility is complex, it is possible for organisations to become competent in handling accessibility across all of their digital products, both internal-facing and external-facing. After all, complexity is not something that organisations are scared of. All product creation is complex. Most things worth doing are complex.

You've already come up with your organisation's answer to, 'Is this complex thing worth gaining competency in?' so the remaining question is, 'Can gaining competency in accessibility be broken down into manageable action steps to implement within my organisation?'

Examples of how *not* to do it

Think back to the RNIB vs bmibaby example in the overview of ISO 30071-1 and you'll see one way organisations handle accessibility: they ignore it. Then it's all hands to the pump on remediation if anyone complains. You need to fix the problem in the process, not the product, to prevent it reoccurring. Otherwise you, like Achilles, will have placed a Band-Aid on your exposed heel rather than have had it seen to properly.

Maybe your organisation is doing 'well' with accessibility. This is likely to be because you are lucky enough to have what I term an 'accessibility superhero' on your staff. Such a superhero is passionate, committed and energetic. To get across their message, they may have hidden everyone's mice on Global Accessibility Awareness Day[1] to force people to have a day of keyboard-only computing. They may have even succeeded in getting accessibility on the organisation's agenda by doing this. And as a result, you're likely to have promoted them to be your 'accessibility champion' and made them the person loosely responsible for making all of your products accessible.

Unfortunately, this is another Band-Aid. For in any large organisation, the accessibility superhero is likely to burn out as they try to make all of your products accessible. Furthermore, either through this burnout or because they want to see if their successful practices will work elsewhere, they may leave your organisation for another in which they can 'save the day' again.

Depending on one person for any competency of your organisation is foolhardy. No organisation that considers a competency essential allows it to reside in a single point of failure. Even if that single point of failure works well, it doesn't scale.

Similarly, outsourcing the accessibility superhero position may turn out to be a Band-Aid. It may solve the scalability problem, but dependency on an outside agency is rarely an economically efficient course of action. And so the 'solution' will be jettisoned whenever budgets get tight.

These aren't the behaviours of an organisation that considers accessibility as valuable. They're behaviours of expediency.

To achieve efficiency and scalability, you need to embed competence *throughout* your organisation – in your policies, processes and staff. Here's a quote from my interview with Jennison Asuncion, Engineering Manager for Accessibility at LinkedIn, talking about what success in embedding can look like from his work at the Royal Bank of Canada:

> 'What we've done is we've said, "Project managers, you have a role to play. Quality assurance (QA) testers, you have a role to play. Developers, you have a role to play. Designers..." etc, etc. "We will be there to train you on what your role is, we will give you the documentation you need in your role, we'll consult and do all that kind of stuff. But as a project lead, you are ultimately responsible for delivering on accessibility.

Our job as the accessibility team is to be your centre of excellence, but what we want to continue to do is build that culture where it's a shared responsibility."

'We have project managers reaching out to us early in the game to come get our assistance so that they can plan for accessibility in their projects. We get developers coming to us early, because they're thinking of using a particular widget in a project and they want to make sure it's accessible. We actually have procurement people now picking up the phone and calling us to say, "Hey, we're about to start an RFP. We want accessibility brought in." Just that whole thing. I know different companies are at different places, and we didn't get there overnight. The team's been around for at least ten to twelve years, so it's taken time. But since I've been there, it's just been amazing to watch how accessibility is really baked in to what we do.'

If that's what success may look like, how could you get there more quickly using shortcuts from others' experience?

Which job roles impact on the accessibility of products?

To embed competence throughout your staff, you first need to look at what job roles within your organisation have an impact on the creation of your digital products. Every person who has an impact on your digital products could be making decisions every day that will include or exclude disabled and older audiences from being able to use them. And there are more people whose job roles impact on your digital products than you may immediately think.

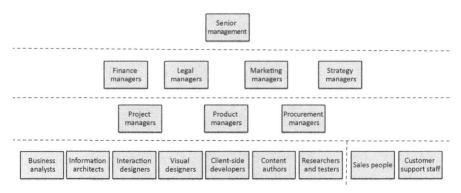

The job roles that impact digital product accessibility

Let's start at the coalface, with the people who actually create the product – its design, coding and content – and those who test the product as it evolves and handle interaction with the community of people using it after launch. Team members with all of these job roles need to be competent and confident about doing *their bit* to make sure they don't drop the baton of accessibility in the relay race that is the creation of the product.

In a relay, each runner needs to do their job right for the baton to successfully reach the end of the race. The baton of accessibility can be passed on in a bad state with poor decisions having been taken, so subsequent work is based on incorrect or incomplete work. Business analysts may specify the requirements for how accessibility will be handled in the product based on bad assumptions from incomplete accessibility user research. Developers may develop perfectly accessible code to implement designs that themselves aren't accessible.

Moreover, a team member may do their job well, but fumble the *handover* of the baton, failing to communicate some aspect of the accessibility decisions embedded in their work to the next team member. Then the next person doesn't understand the aspect's importance and misses it in their implementation.

An interaction designer may design a page or screen layout to clearly segment the product's functionality into different navigational areas, but fail to communicate to a developer the hierarchy behind those segments (for example, as comments in their wireframes in InVision App[2]), so the developer codes them all on the same level. Here the Accessible Rich Internet Applications (WAI-ARIA) specification[3] can be useful notation for interaction designers to clearly and unambiguously communicate these structural semantics of the segments of their design,[4] as well as where the segments should appear on the screen in responsive layouts for different devices.

A salesperson for an online tool could fail to understand the value of mentioning the product's Accessibility Conformance Report (based on the Voluntary Product Accessibility Template®) in its sales materials so potential licensees don't realise it's been created to support accessibility.

Each interaction designer, visual designer, content author, developer, researcher or tester needs to know not only what they have to achieve (ie how to run well), but how to communicate it to the next person in the team who'll work from that to advance the product's creation (ie how to handle the transitions well).

These people, in my experience, are the ones in most organisations who know most about accessibility.

After all, they are the people who almost all accessibility guidelines have been created for. Often they already know what they need to do and may wear their ability to code, design or write content in an accessible way as a badge of competence. But their time, as a resource, is manipulated by those one level above them:

- The *project manager*, who tells them whether or not there is time and money for them to do their jobs in a way that upholds accessibility among all of the other quality measures that are important to the project

- The *product manager*, who tells them what audiences and functionalities the product must support to be successful and deliver the business value of the project

I don't want to play down how important it is for accessibility technology pioneers (like Rich Schwerdtfeger,[5] Steve Faulkner[6] and Bruce Lawson[7]) to get WAI-ARIA and HTML 5 into shape to give us the right technical framework on which to build accessible code. Their work is essential and necessary to enable accessibility, but more work is needed to make people actually implement it in their products.

Accessibility is facilitated or constrained by many people in digital production teams, but most notably by the team's product manager.[8]

Put it this way, who do you think had more impact on whether Apple products include accessibility features: Steve Jobs, or the developers who implemented iOS and MacOS? As Walter Isaacson's fascinating biography of Steve Jobs makes clear,[9] he dictated most of the functionality and look and feel of Apple products; the developers just had to make what he wanted happen.

While both of the 'PMs' I've mentioned can either encourage or inhibit the desires of their teams to deliver an accessible product, most accessibility guidelines are not written in a language that will appeal to them. ISO 30071-1 has been designed to plug this gap, enabling product managers to understand how to balance the costs and benefits of supporting the needs of the product's disabled users with those of all its other users, and enabling project managers to understand how to get the team to deliver on the resulting accessibility priorities that the product manager sets.

Another key manager, whose importance has often been overlooked, is the organisation's *procurement manager*, as many digital products are now assembled from web tools, commercial off-the-shelf software (COTS)[10] or components. And if you're the product manager of a COTS product, you'll only prioritise accessibility over other possible features if you know that procurement managers are going to require this in deciding whether to purchase your software. That's why web procurement standards, like Section 508 and EN 301 549, are as essential to accessibility's future as technical standards like WAI-ARIA and WCAG 2.1.

Above the project and product managers we have the middle layer of finance, legal, marketing and strategy managers. Each of these can encourage or inhibit the product and project managers below them from taking accessibility seriously.

Finance managers can approve or deny budgets for accessibility. *Legal managers* can require that accessibility be taken seriously as a legal risk, or recommend that the risk is too low to bother with. *Marketing managers* can dictate major components of how websites look by setting the brand guidelines for the organisation and its products, and can include or exclude accessibility criteria from the creation of these guidelines. And *strategy managers* can accept or downplay the relative importance of accessibility against a whole host of other harmonising or competing concerns across the organisation's overarching product strategy.

Finally, above all of these people sits a *CEO, MD* or other *executive*. They will set the tone for how accessibility is considered by all those underneath them.

Obviously, in smaller organisations and startups, people will play multiple roles or even all of these roles, but the roles are still the same. For a product to be accessible, *all* of these people need to consistently make decisions that recognise accessibility as an important quality of the organisation's products at all points of each product's development.

The recipe for success in embedding accessibility

Embedding accessibility into the way all these people work can be daunting, because what we are talking about here is organisational change, and that is one of the most difficult things to do in any organisation. We need a way of diffusing this anxiety and making embedding more manageable.

The first aspect of this is to break the task down into its component parts – the components of accessibility maturity:

- Embedding *motivation* and *responsibility* – setting your commitment and budget, then making sure you break down responsibility for accessibility so everyone knows *who* should do *what*

- Embedding *competence* and *confidence* – making sure everyone knows *how* to do the things that are their responsibility via the provision of training and guidelines

- Embedding *support* – making sure your staff have a source of expertise to which they can take questions when their training or guidelines aren't enough

- Embedding accessibility in *policy*, not just *people*, or your policies may hinder rather than help your progress

- Embedding *governance* – making sure you set and regularly benchmark progress against inclusion goals

The final component is embedding in *process* – ensuring consistency of accessibility practice across all digital development projects. This is so important that the whole of this book's companion *Inclusive Design for Products* is devoted to it, and it's summarised in Chapter 5.

The second aspect of making embedding more manageable is to see where you already have some competence in the organisation and build from there, so benchmarking your organisation's current level of maturity against each component is a great way to start. At Hassell Inclusion, we regularly benchmark our clients' competence against all these components to give them an idea of where their strengths and weaknesses lie (their score), where their competitors in the market may score, and what might be necessary to raise their score to a level they are more comfortable with.

Briefly, this is the benchmarking process we take organisations through:

- Introducing the different components to measure their maturity against

- Introducing a simple scale from 1 to 10 for each component, starting from what is required for conformity (score 1 to 3), through what is needed for competitiveness (score 4 to 7), to what is needed for out-performance (score 8 to 10)

- Analysing and scoring the organisation's maturity out of 10 on each component by reviewing documentation (policies, processes and guidelines), interviewing staff to see how that documentation impacts their day-to-day practices, and spot-checking the accessibility of the products that those practices are delivering

- Estimating where the organisation's competitors might score for each component

- Working with the organisation on where they should aim to score for each component – whether they are looking for safety from prosecution, gaining new customers, finding the lowest hanging fruit, or drawing a line in the sand to buy them time while they figure out how to resource a better strategy

- Working with them to discuss what sort of ROI they wish to achieve and how we'll measure that

- Creating a range of work packages that would move the organisation's scores up to the levels they aspire to for each component, with cost-benefits analysis for each

- Agreeing an action plan for which work packages will be done and in what order

The third aspect of making embedding more manageable is to understand that while all the components are necessary, the *order* in which your organisation prioritises them in its planning is flexible. Different organisations can approach implementation differently according to their type (eg public or private), size, product types, users and development methodologies (used to create and maintain their digital products). Often, benchmarking will suggest a way forwards – building on areas where your organisation already has some level of maturity and moving out from there to the other components.

I've characterised the two main orders in which organisations tend to make the necessary changes to become more mature in accessibility in the Hassell Inclusion Way:

- Governance-first (for organisations with lots of digital products):
  Board decision => responsibilities => policies => standards => governance => process => products

- Product-first (for organisations with few products):
  Applying accessibility process and guidelines on one project; if it's useful then doing it on all projects; summarising what has been proven to work in policies; then getting board buy-in to make it official

Let's look closely at each component.

Embedding motivation and responsibility

For an organisation to embed the right practices to ensure that all of its digital products are made to be accessible, staff performing each of the job roles that impact accessibility need to be motivated to accept accessibility as something that concerns them.

There are two ways of doing this:

- Motivating staff directly by providing accessibility awareness training for those performing *each* of the job roles, using a version of the bespoke business case for accessibility document you created in Chapter 3 to share why your organisation cares about accessibility and what priority it has for all your staff

- Motivating those high up in the business: getting them to set accessibility priorities and commission an organisational ICT accessibility policy, and then requiring all staff to comply with that policy with less understanding of the reasons why

The first of these ways of embedding motivation for accessibility within an organisation gains a greater and deeper level of buy-in. My team has helped many organisations achieve this through 'lunch and learn' sessions and larger events marking Global Accessibility Awareness Day. The power of these events is mostly in the 'voila moments' when attendees meet people with disabilities and see them using their products for the first time. It's definitely what we would recommend.

Where the budget is not available to reach everyone's hearts and minds, the second way of doing things can still be effective. And if done well, it is still a massive accomplishment, as many organisations do not consider accessibility seriously at any level other than the web practitioners at the coalface. Most digital products fail on accessibility because no strategy or structure was put in place to ensure it is a value consistently delivered in all the organisation's products.

Hand in hand with motivation goes *responsibility*. Ask who is responsible for accessibility in many organisations and you may get a multitude of different responses from different people – even if people feel that accessibility is part of their job, they may not be sure who is actually *responsible* for ensuring it is delivered in products. ISO 30071-1 requires a department or specified role to be responsible for the organisation's compliance with the standard.

Creating a clear responsibility structure

A good structure for clarifying and embedding responsibility for accessibility within an organisation starts with establishing an accessibility sponsor who will be ultimately responsible for the accessibility of all the organisation's products and practices. They need to be empowered and resourced to delegate this responsibility down through the ranks of the organisation, making sure that those they delegate to are aware of and trained in their responsibilities. And they need to make sure they are monitoring and governing how well staff are fulfilling their responsibilities.

This accessibility sponsor is different from the 'accessibility superhero' role I mentioned earlier. Accessibility superheroes, even departments of superheroes, are usually tasked with all the responsibility for accessibility for an organisation, but given little power, resource or structure to let them safely delegate responsibility, so they end up racing around the organisation trying to influence all the people who actually make decisions that impact product accessibility. And they do this without any ability to get those people to buy in to living up to their responsibility, without any budget to get them the training they need, without any governance mechanisms to check how accessibility is happening across the organisation or any measures to enforce accessibility 'compliance' in the products they are finally asked to test.

In my experience, organisations that handle accessibility well are those with the combination of:

- An *accessibility sponsor* on the organisation's executive board, gaining top-level buy-in for why accessibility is important for the organisation and securing a budget for making it happen, using the business cases in the previous chapter and benchmarking against best practice from organisations that have made their accessibility strategies available (via the OneVoice Accessible ICT: Benefits to Business and Society report[11])

- An *accessibility programme manager* strategically planning and delivering the embedding for which the sponsor has secured buy-in – organising training for staff, providing subject-matter expertise and support for those staff, driving embedding into policies and managing ongoing governance

- Individual *product managers* accepting that the accessibility of the product they manage is fundamentally their responsibility, even though they delegate the details of that responsibility to the individual members of their team

The accessibility programme manager role

The best location for the accessibility programme manager role in the organisation's org chart can be a matter of some debate. ISO 30071-1 suggests it could be part of these roles:

- Chief technology officer

- User experience director

- Digital development director

- Governance manager

Among our clients at Hassell Inclusion, depending on the size of the organisation and the type of digital products that it creates, we've seen the role located in governance and risk, customer service, user experience, development, QA, standards compliance or HR. To give some more public examples: when I was at the BBC my role was located in user experience, having moved from editorial compliance previously. IBM's workplace accessibility strategy worldwide lead reports into the chief information officer, and there's also a chief technology officer for accessibility. At Comcast there's a vice president of accessibility. Microsoft has a chief accessibility officer, and Google and Apple have accessibility directors in senior roles, reflecting the importance of accessibility to them as technology companies.

The important thing to be aware of is that the position of the accessibility programme manager role – or the job role of the person who is given responsibility for it – may fundamentally impact the way accessibility is viewed in the organisation. If accessibility is assigned to someone in legal or governance, they are likely to have a 'stick' approach to embedding it in the organisation with an emphasis on creating unambiguous standards to which they hold staff and suppliers accountable. If it's assigned to someone in user experience, they are likely to take a less formal view, seeing accessibility success more in terms of whether disabled people can use each product. If accessibility is assigned to a technology expert, they may be more interested in embedding accessibility in code libraries. Biases will also come into play if the role is located in corporate social responsibility, HR or marketing.

Each possible location of the role brings its own flavour to how accessibility is seen, and each has strengths and potential blind spots. Accessibility encompasses all of these flavours and all bases need to be covered to fully impact the organisation. The accessibility programme manager can be successful whatever their bias, as long as they acknowledge it and balance it with an appreciation and commitment to the other ways of looking at accessibility.

In practice, the location of the role may be less important than its *continuity*, its empowerment and its ability to flex to survive organisational restructures, including the arrival of new middle managers who may need to be introduced to why accessibility is being taken seriously in the organisation. The direct link the accessibility programme manager has with the executive accessibility sponsor is the key to the organisation's ability to maintain a consistently high level of accessibility embedding and not do what so many organisations have done in the past, which is to flip-flop between times where accessibility is well supported and times where it is badly supported.

To give an example, the Ford Focus 2002 that I drive is one of the most inclusively designed cars in history, but the current 2019 model isn't as a change of line-management of the inclusive design lead in the 1990s saw the new boss emphasise form over function, and the guy who established the competence left the company. At the same time, Ford have a thriving accessibility forum for their digital presence.

Make sure your organisation's accessibility competency is able to withstand changes at the top and the possibility of your accessibility programme manager leaving, through embedding accessibility into your standards, training, policies and processes.

NOW IT'S YOUR TURN

- Ask people in your organisation's digital teams whose responsibility accessibility is, and see if you like what you hear back.

- If you don't have an executive accessibility sponsor, consider how you might go about inspiring one of your board members to take on the role.

- Consider who could take on the role of accessibility programme manager and where the role would be best located.

- Use the accessibility sponsor to find the money and buy-in to empower the accessibility programme manager to drive forward your accessibility strategy.

- Document these things in the organisational ICT accessibility policy template in this book's support materials.

Embedding competence and confidence

Knowing that the only way to sustainably embed accessibility competence throughout the organisation is to delegate and empower product team members to make decisions, the accessibility programme manager will need to source the best training and guidance for them. Unfortunately, most current accessibility training, like most accessibility guidelines, has one major fault: it is too general. It heaps together accessibility issues that concern designers with those that concern developers or writers or testers. And rarely does accessibility training address what project managers or product managers need to know to fulfil their responsibilities at all.

This is one of the reasons why accessibility is considered by many to be over-complex. While it is exceptionally useful and comprehensive, the international standard on technical web accessibility – WCAG – unfortunately structures its large number of success criteria around technical categories rather than the job roles of the people who need to work with them, so people have to read them all.

WAI is working on this via its Silver[12] project, but in the meantime, making accessibility accessible is essential, as Makoto Ueki, Accessibility Consultant at Infoaxia and Chairman of Japan's Web Accessibility Infrastructure Committee, discussed in our interview:

> 'In Japan I've met many people who are sharing the same issue. WCAG 2.0 are well-designed standards. But they're not always well designed for web designers, developers, web masters who are actually using the standards' guidelines to make their web content accessible. This has been my biggest challenge as a consultant, and as chairman of the committee that translated WCAG 2.0 into Japanese – to make accessibility more understandable. Our standards are not easy to understand even for accessibility experts like me. What I'd like to do is to provide a plain-language version of the success criteria to bridge between standardisation and web development.'

To efficiently and effectively embed the right *competence* in your staff, I'd recommend this course of action.

Give your people the right awareness

Start by giving all of your digital production teams
accessibility awareness training to make accessibility
about real people, not guidelines. Find ways
of getting your staff the most vivid, compelling
experience of how different disabled people actually
use your product to give them a 'voila moment',
like the radio presenter gave me in 2008 (see section
'Measure effects' in Chapter 2).

Coming face to face with people using (or not being
able to use) the products they've created in ways
they might never have thought of is incredibly
motivating for your production teams. It's much
easier to understand why you need training if you've
felt the tension between the poor results from your
current level of knowledge and the potential that
you could realise if you built your expertise.

Get your people the right guidelines

Next, find a way of getting your teams the most
appropriate accessibility guidelines for the digital
products that they are creating. Just giving them
WCAG 2.0 doesn't work if they are creating native
mobile apps, for example; you need to find a way
of bridging the gap between WCAG and the native

accessibility guidelines for iOS and Android. I recommend the BBC 'Mobile Accessibility Standards and Guidelines'[13] to help here, as they bridge between web and mobile apps superbly.

Annex C of ISO 30071-1 has useful information on the major accessibility standards for digital products created for different types of device. It also includes links to guidelines that can help organisations 'roll their own' if accessibility guidelines are not yet available for the device they're developing for.

On occasions, an organisation may also want to create their own guidelines if the existing guidelines do not capture the needs of their users sufficiently.

Then make sure the guidelines are as concise as possible and easy to digest and follow by breaking down guidance by job role and converting complex language into simpler language. At Hassell Inclusion, we have created frameworks for some of our clients to do this.[14] Publicly available guidelines like the BBC guidelines also do some of this, and the W3C-WAI's work in progress 'Accessibility Responsibility Breakdown' can be helpful.[15]

Even better, integrate these job-specific accessibility success criteria into the other guidelines you may already have for each job on the production team.

For example, integrate criteria for 'accessible design' as one aspect of 'good design' alongside other criteria, like 'design for readability' and 'design to be memorable', in your organisation's web style guide.

Get your people the right training

The quickest and most effective way of getting your staff to the level of accessibility competence they need is to give them training. While this requires investment, my team's experience is that every penny you spend on training your staff in accessibility saves you pounds later in projects. Accessibility needs to become less about testing things to find what people got wrong, and more about training people to get things right (so tests don't have so much to find). That builds confidence in the whole team.

But do not send your staff on general accessibility courses. Segment your staff by job role and send them on more specific courses which fit their roles (eg accessibility for client-side developers, accessibility for content producers or accessibility for visual designers). Make sure the training gives them all the things they need to do to uphold *their* responsibility for accessibility on projects, and nothing more.

And make sure you only offer training if staff need it. The most valuable resource in a training room is the time invested by the people being trained, so don't train them in anything they already know. Focus on where they need it.

Our experience at Hassell Inclusion, having worked with hundreds of digital production teams in lots of different companies, is that if you ask an employee or contractor if they need any accessibility training, you'll almost always get one answer: no. If a member of staff doesn't know any more than the first thing about accessibility, you can bet that first thing is that if you get accessibility wrong, you can get sued. So they reckon if any of their managers cares enough to ask them if they need accessibility training, they might get fired if they say yes.

We have found that most people have a patchy understanding of how accessibility should impact on their job, having picked up bits of knowledge over the years from the internet, or from the results of accessibility audits, without anyone fully connecting the dots for them. Even people who have been trained in accessibility often find that their knowledge has become out of date as technology and accessibility standards keep evolving. We also often find that people know more about accessibility than they think – they may not know it's called accessibility; they may think it's just 'good web design'.

So, pre-training assessments are essential to know the truth about a team member's accessibility competence – what they know already that is true, what they have picked up that might not be, and where their gaps in knowledge are. We'd recommend doing these whenever you recruit someone or bring together a new digital team.

Successful training is clear on the day and ideally includes post-training certification assessments to see if trainees properly understood the concepts and how to apply them in scenarios that are relevant to their work. For example, competence is not about whether you know WAI-ARIA; it's about what you code if a design requires a date-picker. Certification will give your staff *confidence* to know:

- When they can make accessibility decisions safely themselves – for example, by applying your guidelines to produce the accessible result they want

- When they should call for support from the accessibility programme manager to help them deal with situations they feel may need to go outside or beyond your guidelines

At Hassell Inclusion, we train thousands of people in the accessibility skills needed for their jobs every year. But we believe, like many people, that *training* isn't enough. Professionals need to focus on *doing*. While training helps people *learn* accessibility skills, it's also essential to help them *apply* those skills in their work. *On-the-job mentoring* can help people take their skills and make applying them habitual.

In the end, the value of the training is really measured by whether it has changed trainees' working practices a few months later, enabled them to find defects in their own work and reduced the number of defects being found in audits.

NOW IT'S YOUR TURN

Think about how you can most efficiently and cost-effectively provide competence-raising resources for your staff. This is the approach I'd suggest you take to commissioning your training:

- Audit your staff by job role, considering the level of each role's impact on the accessibility of your products and the staff's current level of competence in upholding that responsibility via assessments. This will enable you to prioritise which of your staff need training most urgently (eg those with the biggest impact and least competence) and how much it is worth spending on that training.

- Adopt a user-centred approach to your training design, ensuring that all your accessibility training is relevant to your staff's needs by asking them about any particular accessibility challenges that come up time and again on the sorts of products they create. Use that information, along with your understanding of their current level of accessibility knowledge and the level that you need them to achieve, to specify the training they require.

- Find a training supplier who not only understands accessibility, but can meet the specification of training you need. It's better to pay for training that you can be sure addresses your team members' needs than waste their precious time with cheaper training – like some free online courses – that doesn't.

- Get your staff *applying* their training in real projects as soon as possible – this not only embeds any guidelines they've learnt in the training in their minds, it also enables them to turn those guidelines into practical expertise.

- Document these things in the organisational ICT accessibility policy template in this book's support materials.

Embedding a support resource

The availability of a support resource to help your staff deal with 'grey area' situations where they feel they may need to go outside or beyond your accessibility guidelines is useful. For efficiency, you need to separate the level of accessibility knowledge you require from your designers, coders, testers and content creators from the level of accessibility knowledge you require from an accessibility specialist who supports them when needed.

My experience is that most large organisations do best when they train all their staff in the basics of accessibility, and train them to identify the circumstances where they should call for support. This second aspect is as much part of their competence in making good, justifiable accessibility decisions (as we will discuss in the next chapter) as understanding how to best apply accessibility guidelines.

Ideally, set up a hierarchy of accessibility support for your staff. They should know:

* When applying WCAG or other accessibility guidelines is *enough* to make good decisions

- When they need to temper accessibility guidelines with *their existing experience* – things that have worked for them on previous projects

- When they should look for expertise (or resources such as reusable accessible code libraries) from *colleagues* in the organisation who have worked on similar projects

- When decisions are so difficult, complex or risky they would benefit from bringing in *an accessibility specialist* for their advice

- When they need to commission further *research* to be able to make a justifiable decision

The sorts of difficult decisions for which your staff may need specialist support include:

- Where the application of the standard technical accessibility guidelines 'just doesn't feel right' for part of the product (see ISO 30071-1 Activity 4 in this book's companion, *Inclusive Design for Products*)

- Where the amount of work needed to implement accessibility for a feature becomes onerous or burdensome, because the cost is a disproportionally large percentage of the total cost of implementing the feature

- Where it's not possible – due to lack of time or resource – to do all the necessary accessibility work, so you need to prioritise work to minimise the *accessibility risk* within the constraints you are working in, quantify the risk and put in place any measures you can to mitigate it (see ISO 30071-1 Activities 6 and 7 in the companion book)

It is the accessibility programme manager's job to identify whether the organisation should recruit accessibility specialists as an internal resource, which can be nurtured and built up over time, or to subcontract this support out to a network of external accessibility support partners (including accessibility trainers, accessibility specialists and suppliers of different types of accessibility testing).

Most organisations start off with bringing in external support, but move towards establishing an internal resource over time, as David Banes, former Chief Executive MADA, Qatar, talked about when I interviewed him:

> 'One of the main things I've been really pleased about at MADA is, yes, we brought in people with a lot of experience in a range of needs over many years. But we didn't just lift the model from the US or the UK and do it here; we tried to blend that with local

knowledge, experience and commitment.
And we were careful to not keep changing
our consultant or it would be hard to build a
sustainable, long-term vision and action plan.
In the end, I think that bringing in people
who will then make a personal long-term
commitment to a business is really important.
You do need to employ people.'

Whether they are internal or external, it is important
that support staff don't 'do' the accessibility work
on products (they're not accessibility superheroes),
but that they advise and support the project staff
to do that work so staff build up competence, not
dependence.

NOW IT'S YOUR TURN

- Consider if you need to recruit an external
  accessibility support resource for your product
  teams, and what type of support would be
  most useful – for example, ad hoc support,
  via a retainer for on-call email response over
  the course of a project, or via regular on-site
  accessibility surgeries for staff to drop in and
  talk through new issues with specialists.

- I don't have space in this book to go deeper
  into the best ways of finding the right
  accessibility support service in a cost-efficient

way; I'd recommend you follow my 'Finding an Accessibility Support Resource' blogs[16] for this. These are based on my team's experience providing such services to Hassell Inclusion clients and my experience as the BBC's accessibility programme manager, recruiting internal teams of accessibility specialists and external accessibility support partners to provide support to the teams in charge of the BBC's 400 products.

- Olivier Nourry's 'Get the Most Out of Your Accessibility Expert' advice from CSUN-12[17] is another good resource in this area.

- Document these things in the organisational ICT accessibility policy template in this book's support materials.

Embedding in policy

Ensuring that all your staff are motivated and competent to make the right accessibility decisions at each step of the creation of a product is a great start to embedding accessibility best practice in your organisation. But you need to make sure that their best endeavours are supported and not overridden by another inhibitor or facilitator: your organisation's established policies, standards and guidelines.

To illustrate the importance of embedding accessibility criteria in the generation of guidelines, let me give you an example of the most common and difficult accessibility problem that organisations face. It's the problem of inaccessible branding and colours.

An organisation's brand is exceptionally valuable, and brand usage guidelines are normally one of the first sets of guidelines that any organisation creates. Depending on the size of the organisation, the value of money spent on the exact shade of blue or pink used in its logo and brand colours is often unappreciated and ridiculed by those outside the branding world. But there are good reasons for these costs, as the logo and colours will be used in thousands of different circumstances, across growing numbers of media channels – everything from radio and TV adverts, to printed collateral, billboards, websites and apps. They need to represent the organisation's values in the minds of the public and achieve the right balance of being distinctive from competitors and yet familiar. It's a huge challenge and expense to get right.

How then should a web manager respond to this common finding from an accessibility audit: 'There is not enough contrast between the text and background colours. This can be fixed by changing the text colour to #DE0079'? If the original colour is specified in the organisation's branding guidelines, the web manager cannot follow this guidance to achieve conformance with WCAG 2.0 AA and keep 'on brand'. They have the unenviable choice of annoying either potential disabled users or their branding colleagues.

I've lost count of the number of occasions when the brand colours of a client's website have fallen foul of the colour contrast checkpoints of accessibility guidelines. The 'simple solution' that the accessibility testers (or disabled people who write in to complain) suggest is not simple in the slightest as a change in the colours might require much of the expensive branding work to be redone.

I'll talk about an accessibility personalisation solution to the colour contrast needs of disabled people that does not require expensive branding changes or deviation of a website from brand guidelines that I created later on in Chapter 6. But the point here is that these difficulties could have been averted if accessibility colour contrast constraints had been included in the brief for the creation of the organisation's branding in the first place.

This is just one example of how your organisation's policies, standards and guidelines – whether written or unwritten – can either facilitate or inhibit your aim of making accessible products, and how including accessibility criteria within the creation of those policies can prevent real and expensive problems occurring every time they are used.

Distribute criteria into existing policies

A common approach to embedding accessibility in your organisation's policies is to create an accessibility policy for your organisation. I've read and written many such accessibility policies, especially in the UK where the Public Sector Equality Duty requires public bodies to create, publish and update Single Equality Schemes every few years. These policies partly comply with ISO 30071-1 by explaining the organisation's commitment to ICT accessibility, but rarely summarise its approach, which is also required.

Unfortunately, I've also found discrepancies between the wording of such policies and what actually happens day in, day out in the organisations that have them. To give a wide multi-agency example, a survey of the Accessibility of Federal Electronic and Information Technology (US) in 2012[18] found that, despite Section 508 of the US Rehabilitation Act requiring it, 'less than 50% of agency components incorporated specific applicable Section 508 Accessibility Standards as requirements in each procurement solicitation'.

I believe one of the main reasons for these discrepancies is that this accessibility policy information is confined to one document, which is reasonably easy to overlook. Creating a central accessibility policy may backfire – it puts everything in one place, so people can ignore it. For your organisation to take most notice of accessibility across its functions and policies, a more effective approach is to embed accessibility criteria across *all* the policies that are important in your business – one paragraph here, a couple of metrics there can make all the difference.

It is not wrong to want a central accessibility policy. ISO 30071-1 advises you to create an 'organisational ICT accessibility policy' where you summarise what your organisation does in this area – most likely because you are required to have one by a set of regulations that cover your organisation. But it advises you to make this a list of links to the accessibility criteria that are *distributed* and *embedded* across your organisation's policies.

Which policies should have accessibility baked in?

With that approach established, you need to consider what the best strategy is for identifying which policies impact accessibility, and then how to embed accessibility criteria in them.

Identifying which policies impact accessibility is facilitated if you have an organisational policy repository from which to work. If you don't have such a repository, this could be because policies are scattered throughout your organisation's departments, or because you don't have any written policies at all. Whichever of these is the case, here's a quick list of some common policies, standards and guidelines that impact the accessibility of an organisation's digital products and its ability to support those products' disabled and older users:

- Overarching digital accessibility goals:

  - Specific goals, based on the goals of ISO/IEC Guide 71:2014, which are detailed in Annex A of ISO 30071-1

  - More relatable targets like 'become the most accessible bank in the world', as long as these are quantifiable

- Design guidelines, such as:

  - Brand usage guidelines

  - Style guides and design pattern libraries the organisation has built up

- Technology policies, such as:

  - Technology strategy – whether the organisation has standardised policies on using particular digital technologies to create its products (for example, whether it creates native or hybrid mobile apps)

  - Browser support policy and assistive technology support policies

  - Any code libraries it has built up

- Procurement policies, such as:

  - How accessibility is mentioned in the organisation's standard templates for requests for proposals or invitations to tender, and procurement contracts

- Standard product-launch checklist

- Governance policies:

  - Checkpoints to monitor how teams are living up to the accessibility goals of the organisation in general and per product (see next section)

- Customer support centre standards, such as:

    - Standard script for dealing with calls to the organisation's customer support centre

    - The 'Frequently Asked Questions' document that it publishes on its website so users can find their own answers to their questions

- Social media guidelines

Once you've identified which policies affect accessibility, prioritise those that have the most impact, identify who owns or is responsible for those policies and use the support of your executive accessibility sponsor to approach the policy owners about how accessibility criteria could be incorporated in their next revision.

NOW IT'S YOUR TURN

Auditing your organisation's policies for whether they need to mention accessibility may seem daunting, particularly in any large organisation that has large numbers of departments with large numbers of policies. My recommendation is that you start your work in those digital policies that most directly impact the creation of your organisation's recent digital products and work back from there into the underlying policies that impacted the creation of those digital policies.

The best place to start is with establishing:

- A top-level business case and resulting organisational accessibility strategy (as we discussed earlier in this chapter).

- A default degree of accessibility that you will aim to achieve for all your digital products. This should be:

  - Easily specifiable and understandable inside and outside your organisation, including to your suppliers and users

  - Flexible and scalable (to make sense across all the different product types you expect to create)

  - Measurable

  - Able to predict the quality of customer experience

  - Achievable (there's no point in reaching for the moon if you don't have the resources to leave the ground)

  - Able to facilitate discussion around exceptions

  - Justifiable (to your senior management and users)

- A standard accessibility section to be added to your organisation's ITT or RFP procurement documents and their counterpart procurement or outsourcing contracts.

- A standard form of words to use in explaining your organisation's accessibility commitment to your users in the ICT system accessibility statement of each of your products (see Chapter 5).

- Policies documenting the organisation's position on some of the key decisions made in the ISO 30071-1 activities, referenced in Chapter 5 – for example, the default assistive technologies and browsers you will aim to support and the default position on accessibility support across platforms.

- Document these things in the organisational ICT accessibility policy template in this book's support materials, where further guidance and examples may be found.

Embedding in governance

Many organisations currently equate accessibility governance with automated tools that constantly check their website against a large number of checkpoints. Increasing numbers of accessibility service companies have such a tool – usually a costly one – that you can procure and use for checking millions of pages for minor slips.

But that 'minor' is the thing. While I don't want to downplay the importance of getting accessibility consistently right on a detailed heading-by-heading image-by-image basis, many organisations get so obsessed with this that they neglect more fundamental strategic aspects of governance, like doing user testing to make sure disabled people are actually able to use the site when the headings and alt-text are in place, and doing this checking over *all* of their sites, mobile apps and social media channels.

While smaller organisations with one website and few social media channels may be able to get away with simple accessibility governance strategies, larger organisations should consider:

- What digital products to monitor

- What accessibility metrics to monitor for on each of those products

- How often to monitor them

- How well to monitor them

- How much it costs to monitor them

- What to do with the results – do you use a carrot, a stick or take no action at all when issues are found?

What digital products to monitor

Start by enumerating all of the different digital projects that your organisation is currently working on, whether they are updated versions of current products, redesigns of current websites or mobile apps, or wholly new ventures. Add all of the digital products that your administration teams are currently maintaining. Then add all of your external channels – for example, your YouTube and Instagram channels, your Facebook and LinkedIn pages, your Twitter account, and any blogs or other off-site mechanisms that you use to communicate with your users.

This is your *digital portfolio*. Consider the accessibility of every product in it and user journeys that cut across multiple products. For example, you may create a blog to provide the details of a new competition; you may promote that via Twitter and Facebook; and you may require users to enter the competition on your main website. Ensuring that your disabled users are able to complete that full journey, through the different levels of accessibility provided by each of the sites and services they will need to navigate, is so much more important than whether one image on that journey is missing alternative text.

Also include all the internal websites and digital tools you use for your staff in this portfolio. And make sure you don't miss digital products that non-technical parts of your organisation manage, like online job application systems or eLearning systems for onboarding new staff, which are procured by HR departments, or anything to do with customer service. Otherwise you may find that you receive complaints about the accessibility of parts of your digital portfolio that your users and staff really value, but you have overlooked as they don't generate revenue.

Categorising products and their level of accessibility

It is likely that some of your products will be more important than others, both to you as an organisation and to your users. To give an example, over 90% of the accessibility complaints that we received at the BBC were for the video-on-demand service iPlayer. This does not mean that iPlayer was an unsuccessful product. The converse was true – the product was so successful that it became an overwhelming reason why people came to the BBC website. As such, it became a *pillar* – a popular product that brought people to the BBC site and gave the BBC the freedom

to create other riskier products and promote them to
the stream of people visiting the pillar.

Other products may be thought of as *enablers* –
pieces of underlying technology, such as sign-on
systems and global page templating systems, that
are needed to provide core functionality across the
whole of the website or websites or make them
run more efficiently. Yet other products may be
innovations – punts or hunches that could turn out
to be either ill-conceived, one-off award winners, or
the future pillars that your organisation will depend
on for your revenues or audience reach going
forwards (most mobile sites are a good example
of this as they started as innovations, but are now
pillars due to mass audience take-up). Then you
have your *standard websites and apps* in the middle
ground – using established enabler technologies to
support common, if not glamorous, user goals, such
as finding company information, help or careers
information. And finally, you may have *short-term
'campaign' sites* that are designed to do a clearly
defined task (such as promoting a new product or
service) for a short time and then be removed from
the portfolio.

Each of these types of product has a different
purpose and lifecycle, and so may reasonably need

to adopt a slightly different approach to accessibility. This is why you need to consider accessibility strategically across the *entirety* of your portfolio:

- Prioritising accessibility for *enablers*, as accessibility deficiencies there will be felt across all your products

- Looking to make *pillars* accessible, as you are likely to get most return on your accessibility investment here

- Ensuring your *standard websites and apps* aren't letting you down

- Giving less attention to *short-term campaign sites*, unless ensuring 100% of your users can respond to the campaign is key to its business aims

You may need to make *innovations* an exception case for accessibility. They may require cutting-edge technologies that by definition are less likely to be supported by accessibility guidelines and assistive technologies. And in the final analysis, they may not connect with *any* of your users at all. But you will need to explain this to your users and make sure accessibility is 'added in' as soon as the product starts to find its audience.

For example, the team behind the award-winning gov.uk site sensibly but controversially held back accessibility work[19] until the ideas behind the site had coalesced, then implemented accessibility brilliantly when the full site was built[20] based on the lessons learnt from the alpha.gov.uk prototype.

Multinational organisations that create specific digital products for different countries may segment their products by *territory*, as they may wish to follow legal requirements for accessibility for each territory in its required level. For example, an organisation may decide that products designed for territories with strong accessibility legislation (such as the United States, the UK or Australia) require better accessibility than products designed for territories with weaker accessibility legislation (such as Brazil, Hong Kong or France).

Your governance strategy should include the full scope of your digital portfolio and may require different levels of accessibility from your products in different categories to contribute to the overall accessibility score for the whole portfolio.

Accessibility assurance metrics

The next question is how to measure that accessibility. I won't go into detail here because ISO 30071-1's Activity 6 (detailed in the companion book, *Inclusive*

Design for Products) will provide all of the strategic information you need. Suffice to say at this point that the metrics you choose to measure are likely to have a massive impact on the behaviour of your staff, who will generally work to meet your metrics rather than your users' needs unless these two things are linked in your metrics-setting process.

Two other important aspects of monitoring are how *often* you monitor against your metrics and how *well* you monitor against them. These two aspects, together with the metrics you've chosen, will dictate how much it will cost to do this accessibility governance monitoring. You need to strike a balance: to achieve total assurance that your organisation's digital products are consistently accessible costs a lot of money whereas lower levels of assurance can be bought more cheaply, so you will need some way of deciding and justifying the budget. And of course, the decisions that you made on your organisation's motivation for accessibility (in Chapter 3) will help you to make these new accessibility governance investment decisions based on well-considered business cases that you've created for your organisation.

All data, no action?

Finally, all of this governance can be robbed of its value if you have not established what you will do with the results of your monitoring. Will the results be a carrot or a stick to those parts of your organisation developing or procuring the products, or will you take no action at all based on your monitoring results?

Accessibility monitoring tools can create impressive looking dashboards that enable senior management to get a handle on how well different parts of their organisation are upholding their accessibility responsibilities. But these are worthless if management aren't sufficiently bought-in to the importance of accessibility to hold their staff accountable when they neglect to deliver the right degree of quality, or potentially deny a product's sign-off for launch if its accessibility is deficient. This again is why it is so important to properly establish your organisation's motivation for accessibility before you start embedding or governing it. An organisation's real values are not those things that it says in its policy documents, or even those things that it regularly measures. Its real values can be seen in the things that it actually delivers and how it treats its users and staff.

NOW IT'S YOUR TURN

Use the organisational ICT accessibility policy template in the support materials for this book to guide you through documenting:

- All the products in your digital portfolio

- Each product's category (and its relative importance)

- The level of accessibility that you expect each product to contribute to the accessibility score for the whole portfolio

- The type of testing needed to measure that accessibility across the different stages in the lifestyle of the product and the budget you will allocate to that testing

How to comply with ISO 30071-1

ISO 30071-1 provides a holistic approach to the accessibility of digital products by combining guidance on implementing this both at organisational and system development levels. Compliance with ISO 30071-1 requires organisations to:

- Address all of the recommendations of the standard and be able to justify any course of action that deviates from these recommendations

- Create the organisational ICT accessibility policy and assign responsibility for compliance with the standard to a specified department or role

- Document their decision processes in each digital product's ICT system accessibility log (in hard copy or electronic media) to provide evidence of following the recommendations and guidance in the standard for each product

At Hassell Inclusion we have helped many organisations comply with BS 8878 and are currently working to help organisations gain compliance with ISO 30071-1. We do this by training accessibility programme managers in what they need to do to be in compliance, acting as consultants to do this work for them, or – as in the case of one UK company[21] – reviewing the documentation that its team members had already created having read the first edition of this book.

While many organisations want to prove compliance purely to be recognised as being best practice, digital agencies and tool vendors pursue becoming compliant with the standard as it enables them to prove to clients that their services, cultures and teams are able to *consistently* create accessible digital products. This gives clients confidence in them as suppliers of digital products and embedded solutions in the long term.

FIVE

Enable Process – How To Embed In Your Digital Product Development Lifecycle Process

This quote from Rob Wemyss – a member of our Hassell Inclusion team, from his time as Head of Accessibility for Royal Mail Group in the UK – summarises what organisations have got to gain from using ISO 30071-1:

> 'The standard has given us a framework to help reduce costs and improve our quality when delivering accessible digital products for our customers.'[1]

You've already seen how ISO 30071-1 helps make accessibility understandable and strategic by providing a framework to embed it within an organisation. It also provides a way of embedding accessibility in your software development lifecycle to help turn it into a user-centred inclusive design process. It identifies the key decisions made in development that impact whether the product will include or exclude disabled and older people across the whole of its lifecycle, situates these as activities which you can integrate into your current process, and provides an informed way of making these decisions and documenting them to capture your best practice.

In this chapter, I'll summarise the activities in the second part of ISO 30071-1 which are detailed in this book's companion, *Inclusive Design for Products*. The activities are based on best practice in embedding accessibility in digital product design gathered from many of the top websites in the world, including my work at the BBC.

As digital products are often created to be used within non-digital contexts – think lift-control panels, ticketing machines or apps to guide people around theme parks – it is important that people creating these *hybrid systems* have ways of working that flow across non-digital and digital design. So the team creating ISO 30071-1 also worked to harmonise it with inclusive design and user-centred design processes for non-digital products.

To give you an example of this, in 2010–11 I represented the BBC as part of a European consortium of organisations exploring how to gain competitive advantage by making products inclusive, led by the Engineering Design Centre (EDC) at Cambridge University. Over the course of the year we proved that EDC's processes could be usefully applied across products ranging from confectionery wrappers to bank branches; from personal medical equipment to consumer white goods.

We also found that the processes, methodologies and tools that EDC had created – the Inclusive Design Toolkit[2] – related closely to much of what my team of digital usability and accessibility specialists were already doing at the BBC. What my colleagues on the programme couldn't understand was why accessibility guidelines in the web space were a technical *checklist*, when everything that they had learnt about inclusive design was about understanding user needs, encapsulating them in personas and using those personas to inform all stages of an iterative design *process*. I used these insights to ensure that BS 8878's process for the production of digital products and ISO 30071-1's activities after that were designed to harmonise completely with the wider inclusive design processes that EDC uses and the ISO Standards for Human-Centred Design of Interactive Systems – ISO/FDIS 9241–210.[3]

As well as harmonising with inclusive design for non-digital products and systems, ISO 30071-1's activities also include user-personalisation concepts that are unique to the adaptable, customisable nature of software. These add a useful flexibility to product development where the needs of one or more sets of users diverge from the needs of the majority of users.

Activities aligned with business intelligence to build a better product

Many people have noted that much of the guidance in BS 8878's steps and ISO 30071-1's activities reflects advice promoted by digital web experts from *outside* the accessibility field on how to build an effective website. Neil Collard, Strategy and Planning Director for e3, in his great seminar 'How shopping for shoes helped change the way we sell financial products',[4] says the things a website needs to be *effective* are:

- To be easily found by its target audiences

- To represent and develop your brand and its values online

- To maximise conversion (by ensuring all your visitors find what they need and become customers)

- To retain customers and drive value (by keeping the site fresh and responsive to the needs of your customers as your business grows)

ISO 30071-1's activities align well with this list, and its user-centred way of thinking about accessibility provides a great way of focusing digital product creation around these important things. ISO 30071-1 is based on a lot of business intelligence which, when followed, should deliver a *better* product, not just an *accessible* one. And this is slowly opening up organisations that have been resistant in the past to accessibility.

As Debra Ruh, CEO and Founder of Ruh Global Impact, USA, put it when I interviewed her:

> 'If we do not embed accessibility at the process level, we will keep trying but failing. However, if we encourage accessibility as part of the design process, we can be successful. Accessibility must be built into the development lifecycle. We build privacy

and security in at the process level, so should manage accessibility the same way.'

It's important to say here that ISO 30071-1's activities do not require you to throw out your current digital development process. They are designed to be embedded within the existing process that you have, whether it's Agile or Waterfall, strict Scrum or bespoke.

Making good decisions

Another essential aspect of ISO 30071-1's contribution to accessibility best practice is its requirement for organisations to make decisions in each activity in a way that is informed, justifiable and transparent.

A huge number of decisions are made across the team of people working on a digital product every day. While ISO 30071-1's activities highlight the *key* decisions made in digital production projects that have most impact on accessibility, all decisions, to a greater or lesser extent, may have an impact. So it's important for each member of the digital production team to be *empowered* to make decisions, to know how to make them *well*, and to know when they should ask for decision *support* from accessibility specialists.

This may seem like teaching your grandmother to suck eggs, but my team has found that it's essential grounding for understanding how to get the best out of ISO 30071-1's activities. It replaces the rigidity of most accessibility guidelines with permission for team members to use their brains in working out how to make a good decision in the context they're in.

ISO 30071-1 encourages team members to be aware that every decision should:

- Be recognised as a decision
- Have all options and their implications considered
- Be made based on justifiable reasoning
- Be noted in the product's 'ICT system accessibility log' for transparency

And it requires team members to do this for each one of its activities.

This is essentially a democratic, empowering way of working. It encourages team members to think carefully about why they are about to do the things they are about to do, whether there is another way of doing things and what the implications are of each. It encourages them to make decisions based on their own understanding of the product and the best available research on its users' needs in the country or culture in which they will be using it.

Fundamentally, it places accessibility back in the sphere of cost benefits like all other decisions made on a project. Understanding that accessibility isn't the only important quality that teams are trying to embed in their product, it enables team members to 'listen to their gut' in dealing with situations where blindly following accessibility guidelines may feel like 'the tail wagging the dog' when the amount of work necessary to make some functionality work for a particular group of disabled people is overwhelming the rest of the work on the project. It also handles situations where fully complying with a set of technical accessibility guidelines is actually infeasible or unreasonable for a particular digital product.

As an example of the importance of this thinking, consider the accessibility of YouTube. The purpose of YouTube is to allow the general public to upload their own videos to share them with anyone who would want to watch them. Two aspects of this purpose provide real challenges to making it conform to WCAG AA.

For a video to be fully accessible, it needs to include captions, audio-description (AD) and interpretation into sign language, but as it is unlikely that users will include such access services with the videos that they upload, video on YouTube can only be made accessible by YouTube itself. But the massive amount of video being uploaded to YouTube every minute of every day makes it both technically infeasible and economically unreasonable for YouTube to be required to provide access services for all of its video.

To give a benchmark comparison, the BBC's 'gold standard' is to provide AD on 20% of all its broadcast programming. And yet, for YouTube to reach WCAG AA it would need to audio describe 100% of its videos. That makes no commercial sense.

The important thing here is the competence to be able to justify your decisions and the discipline to always write that reasoning down.

As Brian Kelly, Director of UK Web Focus, put it when I interviewed him on the importance of being able to bring these practical business decisions into accessibility compliance in the education sector:

'What we're talking about is really a user-centred approach to providing services. What we're saying is you look at the users and you look at their requirements and the challenges in providing these. The difficulty we have is a set of technical guidelines that are great and over time they've evolved, but unfortunately, they've been treated as if they've been enshrined in legislation: "We feel we have to do this."

'Suddenly the user isn't there any longer. It's not about the user. Strict conformance with treating those guidelines as mandatory requirements means services are lost.

'Within a university context, imagine all of those peer-reviewed papers in institutional repositories which are in PDF format and typically do not have alt-tags in their images. What should you do? Do you help to enrich the accessibility of those resources by removing them? That's quite clearly preposterous.'

This lack of understanding of the challenges and costs of accessibility in guidelines and by legislators was perfectly demonstrated in 2017 when the University of California Berkeley cut off public access to tens of thousands of video lectures and podcasts in response to a US Justice Department order that it make the educational content accessible to people with disabilities.[5] While the University said it has plans to create new public content that is accessible to listeners or viewers with disabilities, content that was inaccessible to people with disabilities is now inaccessible to all. That is equality, but I don't think it's a solution to anyone's needs.

Documenting your decisions

ISO 30071-1 requires you to record your justifiable reasons in a document called an *ICT system accessibility log*. This document is an active log for internal use into which each accessibility decision made over a digital product's lifecycle (after launch as well as before launch) is detailed.

This is useful for five reasons.

Firstly, the ICT System Accessibility Log is like the Captain's Log in *Star Trek*. You know the drill: Captain Kirk talks into his Captain's Log before going down to the surface of the planet, most likely to find some sort of crystal that the Enterprise needs to continue 'boldly going where no one has gone before'. He takes down two red-shirted men to the surface of the planet alongside more recognisable crew members. And anyone who's seen the programme knows what regularly happens: when they beam back onto the ship, the two red-shirted men have not made it.

My ideal James T Kirk at this point goes back into his cabin, listens to the reasons for going to the planet surface that he dictated into his Captain's Log and considers whether the expedition was worth losing two members of his crew for. The Captain's Log enables him to revisit the reasons for his decisions after he has got a better understanding of the implications of those decisions.

Being a captain is not easy, and part of the job is to make complex decisions based on incomplete knowledge of what the consequences will be. But a good captain improves the odds in the long term by using their log to learn from their mistakes, whether they were hot-headed, ill-judged, naive or unavoidable.

The same reflective learning is possible, and the maturity of an organisation's approach to accessibility can be easily examined, by reviewing the decisions in its ICT system accessibility logs. This is what 'Iteration is used to progressively eliminate uncertainty during the development of ICT systems' in clause 7.1 of ISO 30071-1 means.

While ISO 30071-1 does not place such an emphasis on conformance as technical accessibility standards like WCAG, it requires organisations wishing to claim conformity with ISO 30071-1 to make their ICT system accessibility logs available for inspection to provide evidence of following the recommendations and guidance in the standard.

Secondly, the ICT System Accessibility Log is like a 'black box' flight recorder. If the worst-case scenario happens and the plane goes down, crash investigators always look for the black box because it contains a recording of the decisions made on the flight-deck in the vital last few minutes before the crash happened. Most of the breakthroughs in flight safety have come from analyses of such recordings – read Malcolm Gladwell's fabulous *Outliers* book[6] to see him prove that.

The worst-case scenario for web accessibility is complaints from users that turn litigious. Here, ISO 30071-1's concept of 'justifiable reasoning' links with the concept of 'reasonableness' that is part of many nations' disability discrimination laws, such as the 'reasonable adjustments' required in the UK Equality Act 2010 and the phrase 'reasonable accommodation' which is included as a general principle under the Americans with Disabilities Act.[7]

Lawyers on BS 8878's writing team who originally came up with the idea considered the link between its principle of 'justifiable reasoning' and 'reasonableness' to be sound, and following ISO 30071-1's advice in noting the justification for your decisions may help present a case for 'reasonableness' if you need it in legal proceedings, but until case law is established that tests the link, the two terms cannot be considered to be analogous.

More concretely, my experience in dealing with accessibility complaints is that most disabled people dislike website owners' failure to consider accessibility much more than being given a reason why the accessibility feature they needed wasn't included, even if they disagree with that reason.

Thirdly, the ICT System Accessibility Log is useful while the project is running as it allows the team – especially its product manager – to keep track of the research conducted and accessibility decisions made on the project. The product manager needs to be able to review quickly whether decisions being made are sensible and justifiable, not just individually (does the decision chime with the accessibility goals of the product?), but also cumulatively (does it make sense

in the context of other decisions already made?).
They need to be able to see any relationships between
decisions – how one decision has prompted others,
or where a decision has been made that undercuts
previous decisions (for example, where a project has
already created or procured a media player that can
play captioned video, but then a decision is made to
not caption any of the video being delivered by the
project). They need to be able to quickly review how
each decision impacts the whole project's level of
cost, benefits and accessibility risk, as this is the key
way of assessing the justification of each decision,
and track the *accessibility risk profile* of the product as
it evolves.

Fourthly, the ICT System Accessibility Log is
essential where you are outsourcing or procuring
the product externally. It becomes the set of written
accessibility requirements that you need to place
in your ITT or RFP document to ensure potential
suppliers know what you expect. It gives you
something to measure suppliers' tenders against
when making procurement decisions, as it requires
suppliers to say how they will do accessibility on
your project, rather than allowing them to trot out
the 'right answer', which most know is 'WCAG 2.0
AA', without understanding what that means for
your product. And it is a great help when suppliers
or product vendors cannot deliver all of your

accessibility requirements and you need to prioritise them to meet project budgets.

Rarely does a product come to market that is perfectly accessible – these are the realities of modern product development. The ICT System Accessibility Log will detail all those pragmatic decisions made where the constraints of budget, resource or launch date have justifiably overridden the risk of not making all aspects of the product accessible.

The fifth use of the ICT System Accessibility Log is in helping to create the *ICT System Accessibility Statement* for the product, which you publish as part of the product to inform its users of the reasoning behind decisions you have made that may detrimentally or positively impact their ability to use it. ISO 30071-1's Activity 7 details how to create this accessibility statement.

Integrating ISO 30071-1's activities into your development process

This may initially seem daunting, but over the last eight years my team has done this with organisations large and small; with multinational corporations consisting of large numbers of geographically dispersed siloed production teams and external suppliers, and digital agencies with a staff of two; with long-established companies using well-embedded production processes, and startups with no written production process at all. The ISO 30071-1 activities are flexible enough to fit within the structure of your process or design framework – whether it's Waterfall or a flavour of Agile. They fit well, for example, in the BBC's published Product Lifecycle Management process.[8]

To embed the activities in your existing process, I recommend you:

- Review your existing development process to work out where each of the ISO 30071-1 activities would most naturally fit. This will get you to an updated 'first cut' process for your organisation.

- Test out your updated process on one non-mission-critical development project to check its fit with your company's culture and products.

- Analyse how well the updated process supported you in delivering the desired level of accessibility in the product.

- Make any tweaks to the process to optimise its fit with your culture.

- Create a case study about anything that was useful, if you have time.

- If the process brought benefits to the project, create a plan to roll it out to your other digital product development projects and monitor its impact there.

ISO 30071-1's eight activities, and the best-practice advice for situating them in your process, are detailed in this book's companion, *Inclusive Design for Products*.

The eight activities are:

- Activity 1: specify the widest range of potential users

- Activity 2: specify user goals and tasks

- Activity 3: specify user accessibility needs

- Activity 4: specify accessibility requirements

- Activity 5: specify accessibility design approach

- Activity 6: ensure accessibility requirements are met

- Activity 7: ensure communication about accessibility

- Activity 8: ensure integration of accessibility in system updates

I'll finish this chapter with a quote from my interview with Jennison Asuncion, talking about how the organisation embedded accessibility in its process when he was IT Accessibility Consultant at the Royal Bank of Canada:

> 'What's neat about the standard that you built, and why I was happy to get on board, is that you understood that accessibility is more than just the guidelines. Naturally and necessarily there's a wrapper around the guidelines. The wrapper can include who's responsible for what. What about the people with disabilities? What do we need to think about for them?
>
> 'You're actually talking about the processes that are necessary to execute accessibility and achieve value from people's best efforts. People need to know to include accessibility in testing, so that means QA. They need to include accessibility in the design, so that means the business systems people and the UI designers. They need to know to budget for it, so that means the project manager has to play their role.

'The project manager also has to schedule the time for the testing. Maybe adding extra time in development if a widget needs to have more time spent on it to be made accessible. So that's how all the different roles fit in – the responsibilities end up naturally having accessibility pieces because we're baked into the process.'

SIX

Measure Effects – How To Measure The ROI Of Your Accessibility Strategy

As Jay Brokamp, CEO of Vya Inc. USA, tweeted in 2014:

> 'Clients do not care about features, benefits or solutions. It is the outcome that matters. Does the outcome help achieve their goal?'[1]

Unless you work in an organisation with the ability to 'print money', like Google or Facebook, the continued success and prosperity of your accessibility programme will be massively enhanced if you can prove that it provides a reasonable ROI to the organisation for which you work or are consulting. Unfortunately, the tools we have for proving this ROI are currently letting us down.

To illustrate the current situation, let's compare the business case for SEO with accessibility from an ROI perspective. If I were an SEO consultant, this is how I would sell my services to clients:

The monetary value to a website of ranking high on a Google search for its most important keywords is well established.[2] I can benchmark your current ranking within seconds by just typing your keywords into Google and finding your ranking on screen, right now. So tell me where you want to rank, and I'll quite precisely tell you how much it will cost to get you there. And I can even give you a 'you don't need to pay me unless I can prove I got you there' guarantee because it only takes a matter of seconds to check my proof by typing your keywords into Google and finding your ranking.

This sort of business case is compelling to many organisations, which is why SEO is such a big industry.

Now compare this with how accessibility consultants sell their services:

The monetary value of making your website accessible is still in debate – I have an idea of the number of disabled customers in every country, but figures of their buying power often clash with figures of their relative lack of employment and their age. I can't benchmark the current number or frequency of disabled people using your site as you have no data to recognise when they do this. And if you'd like me to benchmark your current level of accessibility, it will take me a few days and cost you…

But tell me how many disabled customers you'd like to reach and I'll get you there. The cost of doing this will depend on the purpose of your site, the technology it's built in, how often you maintain it, the size and prior accessibility knowledge of your team, and how you will promote it to disabled people once it's created. This could vary immensely from team to team and product to product. And I can't give you a 'you don't need to pay me unless I can prove I got you there' guarantee because I have no way of showing how many disabled people are using your site, and even proving the site is now more accessible is going to cost you. The more proof you want, the higher the price.

If you had to choose to prioritise between SEO and accessibility, where would you put your time and money?

This is why accessibility consultants currently have to spend so much time educating their clients on the value of the other business cases for accessibility before starting to create a strategy for them. They want to let their clients know how much they are 'winning' because of their commitment to accessibility, but at the moment, accessibility benchmarking tools are just not up to the job of giving them sufficient reliable proof.

Capturing accessibility ROI

It's important that you do everything possible to enumerate and put a value on the *benefits* that your accessibility programme is creating, as well as capturing its *costs*.

In Chapter 3 we outlined some of the benefits you can get from accessibility, but it's worth reminding ourselves of them here in the context of measuring them:

- The *risk-mitigation value of not being sued* (the value of the 'accessibility insurance policy').

- The *value of minimising the cost of handling accessibility complaints after launch*, especially where you can compare the costs of making your product accessible (and communicating that accessibility well) against the (resource) costs of dealing with accessibility complaints the last time you launched a digital product (for example, when you deployed a new 'software as a service' application to your workforce).

- The *PR value of any awards* for your digital product, either specifically for the accessibility and usability of the product, or for the product in general, where accessibility was an aspect that the awards committee considered in their deliberations.

- The *impact of your product's level of accessibility on the value of your brand*. This is difficult to quantify, but where you already do surveys of how your audience feels about your product, either your own customer loyalty surveys on the website itself (like Net Promoter[3]), or through 'rate this app' comments in iTunes/Google Play app stores, you could include and monitor responses to questions around the accessibility/inclusiveness of your product.

- The *value of minimising the cost of customer service*. The economics of digital transformation look like this with respect to the costs of dealing with customer queries in the UK public sector: it costs about 17p to deal with a query if it comes online, £5 if that query is being dealt with via a call centre, and £14 if people actually have to drop in to the Town Hall,[4] so the more accessible you make your online service, the more people you can service using less expensive mechanisms.

Other accessibility ROI measures – such as the impact of getting good at accessibility on your ability to recruit a diverse workforce and the resulting uplift in your teams' motivation to deliver accessibility when they have colleagues that need it themselves – are discussed in the Hassell Inclusion Digital Accessibility Experts podcast on Measuring ROI.[5]

Counting the reach of accessible websites

The most compelling evidence for accessibility ROI is to count the number of people with impairments who use your product and the extent of their use of your product's features over time.

The best publicly available case study for the ROI of accessibility that I know of is Tesco's 'Case Study of the Benefits' of its separate Tesco Access website back in 2001.[6] As Tesco had created a *separate* website for disabled people to use – something frowned upon then and hardly ever done now – it was able to count the exact cost and revenue it enjoyed from having created that accessible site.

As inclusively designed sites have taken over from inefficient separate 'accessible sites', it has unfortunately become harder to differentiate the benefits arising from considering disabled people's needs from the benefits arising from more general usability (see, for example, the benefits arising from accessibility experienced by Legal & General Group, which are mixed in with general benefits from usability testing and market research into customer behaviour[7]).

In an age of ubiquitous Google analytics, where product owners are used to being able to count any number of different things about how people are using their digital products and filter them against inferred customer demographics, there has been no way of including disability as one of the demographics. I've helped product managers look for this data wherever they can get it. We've tried counting the views to a site's accessibility statement. But this is a flawed method of gaining some level of understanding of accessibility ROI. If disabled people only visit your accessibility statement when they find an accessibility defect on your site, counting the number of people who visit that page is actually measuring the number of disabled people who found your site 'inaccessible', not the number of disabled people who have used your site. If that is your measure for accessibility ROI, then it will actually *go down* as your accessibility programme *improves* the accessibility of the site.

More successful has been counting the usage of the disparate accessibility features like signed, captioned or audio-described video on a site. It's no coincidence that the other WAI-published case study for the benefits of accessibility is for video-captioning and transcripts – CNET's 30% increase in SEO referral traffic from Google when it launched an HTML version of its site in 2009 with transcripts.[8] Closed captions are a *user preference*, so you can count the number of people who view your videos with them turned on. Although you cannot rely on this figure giving you 'the number of people who are hard of hearing and using your site', as many people use captions who don't have a hearing difficulty, it's the start of some useful data.

If you provide the transcript of the captions on the same page as the video (so deaf-blind people can use their Braille displays to access the video's content), then you can use standard SEO tools to count whether this has increased the keyword density on the page and rated it higher. And you can use this information to partly explain any increase in traffic to those pages that you experience. While it's difficult to run a full scientifically controlled study to see the exact SEO referral impact of putting transcripts on one page, the anecdotal evidence is already compelling.

The CNET case study gives us a clue to the best way ahead for measuring accessibility ROI. Encouraging users to share their preferences with you so that you can monitor their journeys through your site is the best chance you have of enabling their needs to be considered alongside those of other users in the product manager's understandable preoccupation with web analytics.

What product managers want is to be able to use disability as a demographic filter on top of all the other things analytics count, such as how many people with a particular preference use a section of your site, so that they can understand statistically the most important parts of your product to different types of user. It would be useful to show, for example, how many people with a particular disability fall out of the digital product's conversion funnels and don't complete the key transactions you wish them to achieve on your site (fully purchasing the items in their basket on an e-commerce site or signing up for a newsletter on a blog). This would allow you to start putting a *monetary value* on the loss of revenue caused when a particular group of disabled users is not able to complete a transaction due to lack of accessibility/usability.

How to get disabled users to share their preferences

How could you go about encouraging people with disabilities to share their preference information with you?

The problem is that people with disabilities are currently not incentivised to give you any information on their impairments. Disabled users are just like the general population with regard to their privacy online. We all use the same (conscious or unconscious) cost-benefits calculation whenever a site asks us to reveal something about ourselves, or create a login – if there is something in it for me, some sort of benefit, I'll give you my details.

For example, Facebook wants you to disclose lots of your personal information and publish it on your page, which it can use to drive advertising to you in increasingly targeted ways (the 'cost' of membership). But you likely agree to make that bargain because it allows you to communicate with your friends in ways that would be a lot more time-consuming otherwise (the 'benefit' of membership).

While disabled users may enter into that bargain with you regarding many aspects of their preferences and lives, they can be private about their needs. In data-protection terms, their needs are 'sensitive personal information', the highest category of information security. Many people with disabilities have a history of being discriminated against, so they may be reluctant to give out this information to a website if, for example, they are using it to apply for a job. If they aren't assured that the information will be stored anonymously and only used for their benefit, they definitely won't give it out. So the data you need is locked behind two requirements for disclosure that you need to handle carefully:

- Enabling the disabled user to understand what's in it for them – how disclosing that information will give them a better user experience of your digital product

- Enabling the disabled user to understand that you can be trusted to store this information in a way that is anonymous and only use it to benefit them

In the past, accessibility specialists seemed not to have been able to get past the second of these requirements, acting as if there was no good reason why a digital product should try and work out whether the person using it has any disabilities. So I was delighted to see the results of WebAIM's 2014 screen reader survey, which asked screen reader users if they would be comfortable with allowing websites to detect whether they were using a screen reader, and whether it mattered if that detection resulted in a more accessible experience:

> 'Historically, there has generally been resistance to web technologies that would detect assistive technologies – primarily due to privacy concerns and fear of discrimination. These responses clearly indicate that the vast majority of users are comfortable with revealing their usage of assistive technologies, especially if it results in a more accessible experience.'[9]

This information provides some quantitative support to findings of qualitative research that I did at the BBC – that disabled users might not be as reserved about disclosing their accessibility preference information, or having it detected by websites, as accessibility specialists think.

The subsequent discussion about the findings that raged on accessibility blogs and mailing lists still has advocates arguing on both sides. But I think the path ahead is clear: draw out all of the sensible arguments *against* detecting[10] or asking for accessibility preference information from users, then work hard to find solutions that solve each of those issues, so everyone can get the benefits they wish for. Because the prize is worth it.

As Debra Ruh, CEO and Founder of Ruh Global Impact, USA, highlights in our interview:

'My family – my husband, myself, my daughter (who has a disability) and my son – we're a perfect family for corporations to pursue to buy their hamburgers, their cars, whatever... What we cannot currently prove to corporations is that I will make decisions to buy from them as opposed to somebody else because they did or did not include people with disabilities. Because they did or did not make their website accessible.

'Until we can define that consumer behaviour and get the data out there, even if it's by telling one story at a time, we're going to have a hard time really executing as a community of people with disabilities. We've got to track that data!'

What analytics information is available today?

While we wait for that to happen, let's look at the one place we already seem comfortable in asking for this information – as part of 'style switchers', which gain information about the user's preferences to provide them with a better user experience (eg allowing them to change the text and background colours to their preferred ones). These are one example of user-personalised 'additional support measures' that ISO 30071-1 includes in its Activity 5 (see this book's companion: *Inclusive Design for Products*).

These additional support measures are an obvious gift to analytics – you should be able to count the number of people with certain preferences who use your product. The data has been provided directly by the user, so it should be accurate and they will have given you permission to use it.

And yet, most style switchers don't make it easy for this data to be collected, and organisations rarely ask for it to enrich their analytics. This is one of the reasons why these tools have never been particularly valued by site owners. Most site owners put them on their sites because they can, but if they don't count analytics on their usage, they have no way of checking whether or not the tools are an important part of their site.

This is one of the reasons why it's essential for any accessibility personalisation solution you create or procure to include analytics. For example, the personalisation tool I created[11] includes usage analytics as a core part of its functionality. Just by adding the tool to your website, you immediately enrich your analytics with the ability to track some disabled people's use of your site in an anonymous way that they consent to.

Promote your accessibility

One final thing is essential for your ROI figures, should you manage to reliably capture them, to show that your accessibility programme is helping you 'win' and ensure your hard work has been worth it. But it's something that is still badly understood or researched. I'm talking about promoting the results of your accessibility work to the audiences who need it. And as an industry, I don't think we're very good at it.

If you make your digital product beautifully accessible, it doesn't guarantee you visits or downloads from people in the disabled or older communities. They may become loyal customers if you've made a great user experience for them, but they can't do this unless you find a way of letting them know what you've created for them in the first place. 'If you build it, then they'll come' just doesn't work.

You need to market your products to people in the disabled or older communities like you would to any other audience with common interests.

Unfortunately, it's still difficult to market products to disabled and elderly communities, mostly because the communities are rarely communities; they are often disparate, isolated people.

There is a huge opportunity here. According to Total Retail Report, a mere 10% of marketing budgets is allocated to the boomer audience, while 50% goes to marketing to millennials. A study by the National Venture Capital Association, Ernst & Young and AARP finds advertising spend even lower, stating, 'There's simply a lack of marketing, and that sometimes results in low awareness of cutting-edge solutions by many 50+ consumers.'[12]

To target this opportunity, I'd recommend Michael Janger's blogs[13] as a good starting point to highlight some of the issues and directions in the field of marketing successfully to disabled people. Jonathan Kaufman's 'Mindset Matters: A Call To Action for Marketing Professionals to Expand the Disability Marketplace'[14] highlights how companies from Ikea to Mattel are embracing the disability marketplace and developing strategies to find a language that speaks to a community that is diverse in need and tone. And Marketing Week is now reporting on how brands like ASOS and Starbucks are making moves to cater for people beyond the mainstream and unlock the potential of the 'Purple Pound'.[15]

NOW IT'S YOUR TURN

Use the ICT System Accessibility Log template in this book's support materials to guide you in brainstorming how you will promote the accessibility of your digital products to the disabled and older communities, and what mechanisms you can embed in your practices and products to capture the ROI of your accessibility programme.

SEVEN

Continually Evolve

M y favourite TV show of all time, one that's kept me sane on trips to present on accessibility around the world and kept me writing a few more pages on writing weeks, is *The West Wing*. The mug of quotes sits on my desk. The box sets sit on my iPad. My wife is probably listening to its podcast as I write this.

The abiding appeal of the show could be the exceptional writing, the great acting or the sense of camaraderie under fire when the characters are trying to reach for the impossible. But I think it's captured in the phrase that Jed Bartlett seems to say at least once an episode:

'OK. What's next?'

The ability to keep putting the amazing thing you've just done behind you and step out to try the next new thing, to go further, deeper, higher... That's what this chapter is about. If you're thinking 'We're good at this already, what's next?' then this is for you.

Keeping up to date

Let's start with the threat, the overhead, the thing that may seem like a bind, but is likely to be why all of us got into digital in the first place – the thrill of keeping up with constantly changing technology and its impact on how we do what we do.

The history of digital is that what was impossible yesterday may be possible today. This is why ISO 30071-1 requires organisations to not only maintain the accessibility of a product through its lifecycle, but improve its accessibility wherever possible. In practice this means revisiting any decisions to justifiably limit the delivery of accessibility in a digital product, noted in its ICT system accessibility log, in the years after the product's launch as the high costs or infeasibility of providing full accessibility may not still be the case.

To give an example, take the advances happening in AI which are being applied to the automatic creation of captions for videos uploaded to YouTube[1] and alt-text for images uploaded to Facebook.[2] You may remember our discussion on the feasibility of YouTube complying with WCAG 2.0 AA in the section on 'Making good decisions' in Chapter 5. There I said that this was infeasible and unreasonable. That still may be the case, but similar innovations that are producing automated captions on YouTube right now (of varying but ever-increasing quality) may be able to handle the much harder task of automating audio-description (AD) at some point, which may just shift that infeasibility needle further.

At the same time as the capabilities of technology are evolving, our understanding of the access needs of people with disabilities or who are older, and the guidelines that try to encompass those needs, are also evolving. In 2019, while most organisations are still working out what to do with the new WCAG 2.1 Guidelines, it's worth noting that WCAG 2.1 is not the end of the story. The W3C Accessibility Guidelines Working Group charter[3] states that it intends to produce updated guidance for accessibility 'on a regular interval'. This is because accessibility guidelines are really just collections of the most important user needs that experts have discovered through research and user testing products with people with disabilities, combined with suggested technical solutions (techniques) that have been found to meet those needs. WCAG 2.0, 2.1, 2.2 or 3.0 are just snapshots of the best guidelines at any given time that invited experts could agree are useful. And because people are involved in the process to agree on the guidelines, while the guidelines will always be a great reference, they are never likely to be perfect and they are never likely to be complete.

Changes are happening across all layers of the *accessibility ecosystem* at the same time, from standards and assistive technologies to the accessibility of content management systems and JavaScript libraries. See my State of Accessibility in 2019[4] blogs to get a feel for the rate of change.

In digital, the only constant is change.

To keep up to date, it is worth being part of a community where advances in accessibility and assistive technologies are shared. This could be an email list where your organisation's accessibility champions keep each other up to date. It could be keeping yourself up to speed with the #a11y hashtag on Twitter. Or it could be organising a monthly accessibility forum where experts give you presentations on new technologies, standards and directions in technology, and how they may provide opportunities or threats to the way your organisation currently implements digital accessibility.

Optimising your methods

At the same time as advances are happening in technology, advances could also be happening in methods for implementing and achieving digital accessibility, like design thinking and optimisation of processes and policies (such as offered by ISO 30071-1), so it's important that when you're mature in your accessibility methods and practice, you constantly look to optimise that practice.

I'd encourage you to become obsessive about efficiency in your accessibility methods. It's my experience that organisations often spend their accessibility budgets in inefficient places, for example on audits rather than in training QA testers, which would provide much better short- and long-term benefits, or short-term fixes (like accessibility overlays[5]) when actually investing in updating their codebase would be cheaper in the long run. Even organisations that have implemented most of the requirements of ISO 30071-1, which will make it cheaper and easier to sustain accessibility, could usually benefit from implementing the rest. In the same way as it's useful to look at the 'total cost of ownership' of a printer – which includes not just the loss-leader price of the printer, but also the running cost of the ink, toner, drum etc – I believe it's also useful to look at the 'total cost of accessibility' to your organisation.

Over the years at Hassell Inclusion, we have developed a model of the impact of various accessibility 'interventions' on this total cost of accessibility for the different types of organisations that we have supported. Some examples in our model include:

- The likely impact of various types of training or the creation of accessible component libraries on the number of accessibility bugs in different types of product, and a comparison of the cost of training or library creation with the cost of finding and fixing those bugs

- The impact of doing user testing with people with disabilities on minimising the possible PR costs of having to defend your product's accessibility in public

- The benefits of having trained your staff to look for opportunities for accessibility innovation in user research

- The possible cost of doing nothing about accessibility and hoping to get away with it

The model also looks at the cost benefits of evolving from being dependent on external experts for various elements of your accessibility support (especially audits and on-site support) to growing that expertise within your organisation. If this is important to you, it is useful to partner with accessibility companies that believe in your empowerment so they will be looking to facilitate this growth in your staff from day one.

As good accessibility experts are still relatively rare and hard to recruit, the model looks deeply at the cost benefits of building your own second tier of experts from people in your organisation who have become passionate about accessibility through training and applying what they've learnt. At Hassell Inclusion we have run programmes for organisations to create these accessibility champions with great effect.

I'd suggest working with experts to examine which types of interventions you haven't done that would minimise the total cost of accessibility for your organisation is a sensible thing to do. And monitoring that the interventions you have invested in are having the impact they promised is essential, such as tracking the number of accessibility issues that audits find in your products over time, to see if your training is having the right effect.

Those are just a few pointers for spending your accessibility budget in areas that will best impact your business. Saving money where you can, gives you budget to spend on more interesting and creative opportunities for accessibility...

Innovation – moving technology forwards via inclusion

Finally, we'll come to the opportunity that getting good at accessibility can deliver to you – your chance to have an impact on the evolution of technology, to lead the way through innovation breakthroughs.

We've already examined some of the innovations that can result from creative people engaging with the needs of those with disabilities: the trail that led from prototype gesture interfaces for people with communication difficulties through rehab solutions for those who'd had strokes to mainstream VR experiences in Chapter 2, and historic innovations prompted by disabilities such as the typewriter and telephone in the business case for innovation in Chapter 3.

Spend five minutes googling 'accessibility innovation' now and you'll find everything from Microsoft committing $25 million over five years to its AI for Accessibility program,[6] to Apple including Voice Control as a fundamental part of the latest versions of MacOS and iOS[7] (rather than a costly assistive technology add-on). Similar Dragon speech recognition technology[8] has been available on MacOS for so long that I wrote the first draft of the first edition of this book using it in 2014, and Google created Voice Access as an app for Android in 2016. The key thing here is that a niche technology is becoming adopted in the mainstream as it is being promoted to and will hopefully capture the imagination of a much wider group of users. Voice Access is just the latest in a host of accessibility technologies that have achieved this. That's what Apple, Microsoft and the other tech companies are banking on.

The big question, as I asked in the preface to this second edition, is whether this type of innovation is just for the big tech companies that create operating systems and assistive technologies for the rest of the market to use? What does this mean for organisations that aren't tech companies, but use digital channels to sell their products? Or for digital agencies that are looking to find USPs to differentiate themselves from their competitors? Are there opportunities here to be grasped?

I believe there are.

Here are two examples of how my team have been able to help different organisations to consider the innovation possibilities that come from accessibility:

- A digital agency in the UK asked us to help it investigate whether intentionally taking time to better understand disabled people's needs, along with developing tools and skills to efficiently and creatively meet those needs, could encourage its teams to think differently and deliver greater innovations in its products and proposals to clients. If you are looking to discover the future of retail, banking or entertainment, this type of thinking could be a USP and could provide the sort of fresh opportunities that help you retain your best staff.

- A multinational bank asked us to help it propose and deliver an innovative graph sonification system to allow blind people to get the complex information they need to make stock trading decisions in roughly the same time as sighted people. The resulting good practice not only delivered a solution needed by blind people, it was also praised by people who didn't have any vision impairments as being fresh and interesting.

I hope the expansion of the scope of ISO 30071-1 beyond BS 8878's web and mobile apps will encourage more organisations to look into the innovation possibilities that engaging with the needs of people with disabilities may suggest in the newer areas of AI, chatbots, autonomous vehicles, smart cities and the internet of things. There are lots of opportunities to radically impact the lives of people with disabilities if we want to take them, as this quote from Taylor Welling's article 'Reflecting on "good" product design and accessibility' challenges us:[9]

> 'If we want to innovate and add value to people's lives, why aren't we focusing more of our attention on designing for those with frequently overlooked and unmet needs?'

I, like Microsoft and many others, think that if we do this, the world will be a much better place. For all of us.

EIGHT

The Future Of Digital Accessibility

Welcome to the Gold Rush

The importance of digital accessibility and inclusive design has grown hugely since the first edition of this book.

Even in 2014, the demand for people who understand how to make digital products inclusive to everyone was going up and up – you only had to look on job boards on Twitter or LinkedIn to see the world's top companies advertising large numbers of accessibility-related roles, from unit testers to strategic programme managers.

This demand for expertise has increased since then as accessibility has become more mainstream. The race between Apple and Google to add more accessibility features as standard to their mobile operating systems has moved beyond mobile to wearables. And Microsoft is investing in accessibility big time across all of its key products, like Office and Skype. Key internet players like Facebook, LinkedIn and Twitter are now really engaging with accessibility. Google even goes to the trouble of inviting forty experts like myself from all over the world to regular global accessibility summits to advise on its work to make all of its products consistently accessible.

This demand is being fuelled by a global move towards inclusion. As of 2019, 161 nation states had signed up to the UN Convention on the Rights of Persons with Disabilities.[1] This is the first step towards them creating anti-discrimination laws that include access to digital products and services, which creates demand for accessibility guidelines and services so that digital product creators are able to live up to those laws.

While the creation of WCAG 2.0 was mostly a push from accessibility evangelists to get industry to take web accessibility more seriously, the 'push' has slowly turned into a 'pull', evidenced by a growing clamour from industry for clearer guidelines for handling the accessibility of mobile web and app user experiences such as WCAG 2.1. Organisations are increasingly buying in to the evangelists' message on the importance of accessibility. But the accessibility community needs to keep up with the industry's rate of innovation, or accessibility will continue to lag behind.

As the demand for accessibility grows, we need to train more digital professionals in accessibility. This is what my team at Hassell Inclusion is increasingly devoting time and resources to. While supporting individual products in our clients is important, nothing beats the impact of training people across product teams to do that themselves. Great initiatives like Teach Access aim to embed accessibility in university curricula,[2] and freely available massive open online courses (MOOCs) like Google's Web Accessibility training course[3] are helping developers make their first steps in accessibility at zero cost.

There are signs that the accessibility industry is slowly maturing – see my SlideShare '7 Signs of maturing in accessibility & inclusion'.[4] But we also need to make accessibility more embedded, more scalable and more efficient. There is no other way we are going to be able to require more or all of our technologies to be accessible. There are simply not enough accessibility consultants in the UK, for example, to be able to test and fix the estimated 70% of websites that aren't accessible.[5]

And make no mistake – this is absolutely necessary. 'Digital by Default' is not just the slogan of the UK Government Digital Service, but the direction in which most businesses are going. So it is imperative for society that we make sure no one is left behind. 'Including your missing 20%' is not just about maximising your organisation's potential to make money from digital; it's about ensuring no one is excluded from the future of products and services.

While much of the Western world is still paying lip service to the particular needs of older people in using the web, NTT DoCoMo in Japan is not alone in its far-sighted desire to see 'universal design' become common practice in product design.[6] This needs to happen in advance of us reaching a tipping point in demographics arising from an ageing population.

The clock is ticking...

Including your missing 20%

Digital devices, products and the internet have done a huge amount over the last twenty years to benefit disabled and older people – see my accessibility innovation heroes gallery for some of the people who should be thanked.[7] And there are many more interesting technologies coming along that will continue to transform our lives.

Devices are becoming more and more *personal*: from the gesture technologies I've been working with[8] and wearable techs that continually monitor our well-being[9] and place screens closer to our eyes than ever before,[10] to brain-machine interfaces and nano-machines that work around or inside us, integrating technology with our biology.[11]

Devices are becoming more and more *powerful* and *pervasive*: our personal devices put the vast power of the cloud at our fingertips, augmenting our processing capabilities as well as our entertainment opportunities; and intelligent chatbots may soon perform tasks for us as increasing numbers of everyday physical objects become networked through the internet of things.[12]

All of these technological marvels have the potential to enable or disable people with impairments; to be a threat to their continued ability to be informed and engaged members of society, or to be the opportunity that they've been hoping for to engage more fully than they'd ever dreamed possible. The future can be a more enabling place for everyone. It's up to all of us who create digital products and content, whether we're designing a multimillion-dollar cloud service or posting cat videos, to 'include our missing 20%'. Otherwise, they really will be disabled from living in the same brave new world as the rest of us.

Why embedding digital accessibility is critical to our future

Unsurprisingly, my view is that the only way we can handle the growing demand for accessibility is via embedding the sorts of competence in this book in all our organisations. The time has gone when we could get away with web accessibility being an 'add-on' or 'niche'; it cannot then be as effective as it needs to be, even if it becomes a more appreciated professional ghetto. For us all to ensure we design for our future selves, we must make accessibility a key value at the heart of every digital product we create – alongside privacy, security, stability and availability. We must make it 'just the way we do things' for each person to play their part, consistently, repeatedly, in making products accessible. Or else the technology the generation after us creates may exclude us too.

What's Next?

So those are my thoughts... What do *you* think? Are you going to create opportunities to including your missing 20%?

Now that you've read this book, I hope that you wish to join the increasing number of organisations, product owners and accessibility advocates who are working towards a future of more inclusive digital products. I've aimed in this book to teach you the *theory* behind setting up an accessibility strategy for the products you're creating in the organisations where you're creating them. I hope you now feel motivated, empowered, competent and confident that you can start *doing* that. To go deeper into how to embed accessibility in your product process, please go on to read this book's companion, *Inclusive Design for Products*.

I'd encourage you to resolve to become a master at *implementing* that theory, like some of the people I've interviewed for this book. Seek out opportunities to implement ISO 30071-1 across many different projects (and organisations, if you're inclined towards consultancy). Seek out mentoring from people who have been there before you in how to deal with the specific challenges of each project, product and organisation. And keep up to date with accessibility thought leaders, as the nature of digital is that there's always something new happening, and accessibility is no different from that.

Accessibility is a journey.

Thanks for coming with me a few more steps along that path.

Here's to your next steps!

Get help for the rest of your journey from:

http://qrs.ly/3a4a6bm

And please let me know if I can help you further.

– **Jonathan Hassell**
www.hassellinclusion.com

References

Chapter 2

1 https://hassellinclusion.com/blog/rnib-bmi-baby-accessibility
   -lawsuit/
2 http://en.wikipedia.org/wiki/Achilles'_heel
3 http://en.wikipedia.org/wiki/Sam_Farber

Chapter 3

1 https://trendwatching.com/quarterly/2018-11/5-asian-trends-2019
2 https://gov.uk/equality-act-2010-guidance
3 https://mediapost.com/publications/article/336177/baby-boomers
   -spend-more-than-millennials-yet-ar.html
4 www.ons.gov.uk/peoplepopulationandcommunity
   /populationandmigration/populationestimates/articles
   /overviewoftheukpopulation/november2018
5 https://fivethirtyeight.com/features/what-baby-boomers
   -retirement-means-for-the-u-s-economy
6 http://ada.gov/2010_regs.htm
7 https://gov.uk/guidance/accessibility-requirements-for-public
   -sector-websites-and-apps
8 https://un.org/development/desa/disabilities/convention-on-the
   -rights-of-persons-with-disabilities.html
9 https://humanrights.gov.au/our-work/disability-rights/standards
   /world-wide-web-access-disability-discrimination-act-advisory
10 https://hassellinclusion.com/blog/netflix-captioning-settlement
11 https://hassellinclusion.com/blog/web-accessibility-ruinous
   -obligation
12 http://senat.fr/leg/tas04-018.html (page is in French)
13 https://w3.org/WAI/policies
14 http://transition.fcc.gov/cgb/dro/cvaa.html

15 http://globalaccessibilitynews.com/2014/07/14/new-rules-require
-closed-captioning-of-online-video-clips
16 http://deque.com/air-carrier-access-act-update
17 http://legislation.gov.uk/ukpga/1995/50/part/III
18 https://blog.usablenet.com/2018-ada-web-accessibility-lawsuit
-recap-report
19 https://dralegal.org/case/national-federation-of-the-blind-nfb-et-al
-v-target-corporation
20 https://humanrights.gov.au/our-work/disability-rights/bruce
-lindsay-maguire-v-sydney-organising-committee-olympic-games
21 https://lflegal.com/category/accessibility-laws-and-regulations
/legal-updates
22 https://aodaalliance.org/category/enforcement/
23 http://legislation.gov.uk/ukpga/2010/15/part/11/chapter/1
24 http://mcss.gov.on.ca/en/mcss/publications/accessON/policies
_over50/toc.aspx
25 https://pubext.dir.texas.gov/portal/internal/resources
/DocumentLibrary/Policy%20Driven%20Adoption%20of
%20Accessibility.pptx
26 http://slideshare.net/jonathanhassell/policy-driven-adoption-csun
-final
27 https://dl.acm.org/citation.cfm?id=2207736
28 www.official-documents.gov.uk/document/cm76/7650/7650.pdf
29 https://theguardian.com/music/2019/jan/04/beyonce-parkwood
-entertainment-sued-over-website-accessibility
30 https://theverge.com/2018/7/25/17611488/microsoft-xbox-adaptive
-controller-unboxing-packaging
31 https://apple.com/accessibility
32 https://hassellinclusion.com/blog/web-accessibility-ruinous
-obligation
33 https://wearepurple.org.uk/the-purple-pound-infographic
34 https://minoritymarketshare.com/resources.htm
35 http://w3.org/WAI/bcase/resources#cases
36 https://blog.usablenet.com/accessibility-and-seo-wheres-the
-overlap
37 https://section508.gov/manage/laws-and-policies
38 http://mandate376.standards.eu/standard
39 https://itic.org/policy/accessibility/vpat
40 https://hassellinclusion.com/blog/bs8878s-one-year-anniversary
41 http://web.mit.edu/~mcyang/www/papers/2014-morenoEtalb.pdf
42 http://site.xavier.edu/polt/typewriters/tw-history.html
43 https://britannica.com/biography/Alexander-Graham-Bell
44 http://kurzweiltech.com/kcp.html and https://pdfs
.semanticscholar.org/4579/1ac8b2a99f1c80946f1e046633e7289cb96b
.pdf

45 https://youtube.com/watch?v=GyFqZtKvyao and https://www
    .zombiesrungame.com
46 http://slideshare.net/jonathanhassell/accessibility-innovation
    -through-gestural-and-signlanguage-interfaces-32684441
47 https://hassellinclusion.com/blog/accessibility-roi-podcast

Chapter 4

1   https://globalaccessibilityawarenessday.org
2   https://invisionapp.com
3   http://w3.org/TR/wai-aria
4   http://spotless.co.uk/insights/accessibility-information-architects
5   http://elearningcouncil.com/interviews/introduction-to-wai-aria
    -with-rich-schwerdtfeger-ibm-cto-accessibility
6   https://twitter.com/stevefaulkner
7   http://www.brucelawson.co.uk
8   http://mindtheproduct.com/2011/10/what-exactly-is-a-product
    -manager
9   http://techcrunch.com/2011/12/16/keen-on-walter-isaacson-was
    -steve-jobs-a-tyrant-tctv
10 http://en.wikipedia.org/wiki/Commercial_off-the-shelf
11 https://members.businessdisabilityforum.org.uk/media_manager
    /public/86/Resources/Accessible%20ICT%20-%20Benefits%20to
    %20Business%20and%20Society.pdf
12 https://docs.google.com/presentation
    /d/1YjaxD3qNAUVodcx485AyEpq5RY_WpXgFk27TozDbPM8/edit
    #slide=id.g1bc39f4a94_0_6
13 http://bbc.co.uk/guidelines/futuremedia/accessibility/mobile
    _access.shtml
14 https://www.hassellinclusion.com/blog/wcag-2-1-whats-in-it-for
    -you
15 http://w3.org/community/wai-engage/wiki/Accessibility
    _Responsibility_Breakdown
16 https://hassellinclusion.com/blog/accessibility-accreditation-value
17 http://slideshare.net/OlivierNourry/get-the-most-out-of-your
    -accessibility-expert
18 http://ada.gov/508/508_Report.htm
19 https://gds.blog.gov.uk/2011/05/06/accessibility
20 https://gds.blog.gov.uk/2014/01/09/what-are-we-doing-about
    -accessibility
21 https://hassellinclusion.com/case-studies/bs8878-compliance

Chapter 5

1 http://slideshare.net/jonathanhassell/case-studies-of
   -implementing-bs-8878-csun-2012-12145101/31
2 http://inclusivedesigntoolkit.com
3 http://iso.org/iso/catalogue_detail.htm?csnumber=52075
4 Seminar no longer available online, interview with Neil at: https://
   calvium.com/interview-with-neil-collard-from-bristol-agency-e3
5 https://insidehighered.com/news/2017/03/06/u-california-berkeley
   -delete-publicly-available-educational-content
6 https://en.wikipedia.org/wiki/Outliers_(book)
7 http://eeoc.gov/policy/docs/accommodation.html#general
8 https://www.bbc.co.uk/blogs/bbcinternet/2011/04/making_the
   _right_products_in_t.html

Chapter 6

1 https://twitter.com/JayBrokamp/status/451479083268833280
2 see http://training.seobook.com/google-ranking-value for a start
3 http://netpromoter.com
4 https://youtu.be/XBP0EX7vB7U?t=936
5 https://hassellinclusion.com/blog/accessibility-roi-podcast
6 https://w3.org/WAI/business-case/archive/tesco-case-study
7 https://w3.org/WAI/business-case/archive/legal-and-general-case
   -study
8 https://w3.org/WAI/bcase/resources.php/www.w3.org/bcase
   /target-case-study
9 http://webaim.org/projects/screenreadersurvey5/#srdetection
10 Google 'screen reader detection 2014' and you'll find at least six,
   mostly well-considered, views at the top of the search results
11 http://restylethis.com
12 https://mediapost.com/publications/article/336177/baby-boomers
   -spend-more-than-millennials-yet-ar.html
13 http://jangermarketing.com/blog
14 https://forbes.com/sites/jonathankaufman/2019/06/17/mindset
   -matters-a-call-to-action-for-marketing-professionals-to-expand-the
   -disability-marketplace
15 https://marketingweek.com/2019/02/06/how-brands-are-being
   -more-inclusive-for-people-with-disabilities

Chapter 7

1 https://support.google.com/youtube/answer/6373554?hl=en-GB
2 https://facebook.com/help/216219865403298?helpref=faq_content
3 https://w3.org/2017/01/ag-charter

4   https://hassellinclusion.com/blog/category/accessibility-in-2019
5   https://overlaysdontwork.com
6   https://techcrunch.com/2018/05/07/microsoft-commits-25m-to-its
    -ai-for-accessibility-program
7   https://applemust.com/wwdc-apple-voice-control-what-is-it-and
    -what-does-it-do
8   http://nuance.co.uk/dragon/index.htm
9   https://uxdesign.cc/reflecting-on-good-product-design-and
    -accessibility-ac624aeocdba

Chapter 8

1   www.un.org/disabilities/documents/maps/enablemap.jpg
2   http://teachaccess.org
3   https://eu.udacity.com/course/web-accessibility--ud891
4   http://slideshare.net/jonathanhassell/7-signs-of-maturing-in
    -accessibility-and-inclusion
5   https://huffingtonpost.co.uk/damiano-la-rocca/website
    -accessibility_b_9931304.html
6   http://accessinghigherground.org/handouts/ephox/G3ict_Ephox
    _Web_Accessibility_for_Better_Business_Results.pdf
7   http://slideshare.net/jonathanhassell/accessibility-innovation
    -through-gestural-and-signlanguage-interfaces-32684441
8   http://slideshare.net/jonathanhassell/accessibility-innovation
    -through-gestural-and-signlanguage-interfaces-32684441/42
9   https://apple.com/ios/ios8/health
10 www.google.com/glass
11 http://huffingtonpost.com/2013/06/18/mind-uploading-2045
    -futurists_n_3458961.html
12 http://en.wikipedia.org/wiki/Internet_of_Things and http://
    mashable.com/2014/01/13/what-is-nest

Acknowledgements

A book such as this is never the work of a lone
writer. I am indebted to a huge number of
people who have inspired me and given me the
opportunity to build up the knowledge that I've
aimed to share in this book.

Though I am sure I will forget someone, I'd like to
especially thank the following people:

- God, for making it all happen

- My wife Rosnah for being my best friend,
  inspiration, strategist, confidante and touchstone

- My son Robbie for giving up being read
  numerous books at bedtime so that Daddy could
  lock himself in a room and write his own book

- My great team at Hassell Inclusion for their dedication to our common passion and their great conversations to sharpen up the ideas in this book

- Our Hassell Inclusion clients, whose engagement with accessibility and with ISO 30071-1 and BS 8878 keep us learning every day

- Val, Norman and Moya for arranging and hosting my writing retreats so graciously

- All of my interview contributors – experts in my Hassell Inclusion team, Andrew Arch, Graham Armfield, Jennison Asuncion, David Banes, Lainey Feingold, Brian Kelly, Jeff Kline, Axel Leblois, Sarah Lewthwaite, Debra Ruh, Makoto Ueki, Rob Wemyss, Richard England and Martin Wright – for their time and insights

- Rachel Sweetman, for checking all my references

- The Silverton Road 'Dream Journey' crowd in whose company the idea for the video blogs accompanying this book arrived

- My co-editors of 30071-1, Jim Carter and Andy Heath, and the members of ISO/IEC JTC 1, Information technology, Subcommittee SC 35, User interfaces for their insights and dedication to help take a British Standard and make it work internationally

- My IST/45 committee at BSI, who brought their considerable expertise, passion and stamina to our three-year journey to BS 8878

- Richard Titus, who shared my vision for bringing the usability and accessibility disciplines together and hired me to do just that at the BBC

- My team of usability and accessibility specialists at the BBC for joining me on my initial journey in accessibility with such good humour and skill

- Anne Eastgate and Derek Butler, who gave me the time and money to research deep into the needs of disabled children and create the solutions and techniques that are still the underpinning of all my innovation work

- Martin Wright, Richard England and the Gamelab crew for being my partners in innovation and always seeing a challenge as an opportunity

The Author

Professor Jonathan Hassell is one of the top digital usability and accessibility thought leaders in the world. He has over eighteen years' experience in identifying new directions and challenges in digital accessibility, finding best-practice process and technology solutions to these challenges, authoring international standards and presenting best practices to conference audiences across the world.

He is the lead author of ISO 30071-1 and BS 8878.

Jonathan also leads Hassell Inclusion's team of accessibility experts providing strategic accessibility transformation services to organisations worldwide.

He specialises in training and consultancy to embed accessibility strategically within the software development lifecycle process, leadership of innovative digital projects to make inclusion easier and cheaper to implement, and creation of best-practice international web standards.

He is the former Head of Usability and Accessibility, BBC Future Media, where he combined usability and accessibility disciplines to embed inclusive user-centred design across web, mobile and IPTV product creation. He has won awards for product managing the accessibility features of 'BBC iPlayer', the accessibility personalisation tool 'MyDisplay', the accessibility information site 'My web my way', the 'uKinect' Makaton sign language games and the 'Nepalese Necklace' mobility games for blind and partially sighted children.

He, his wife Rosnah and their son Robbie make their home in the 'garden of England', Kent.

You can find Jonathan online at:

⊕ www.hassellinclusion.com
𝕏 @jonhassell
🔗 linkedin.com/in/jonathanhassell